THE FEDERAL FIRE PREVENTION AND CONTROL ACT AUTHORIZATION

HEARING

BEFORE THE

SUBCOMMITTEE ON SCIENCE

OF THE

COMMITTEE ON SCIENCE, SPACE, AND TECHNOLOGY U.S. HOUSE OF REPRESENTATIVES

ONE HUNDRED THIRD CONGRESS

SECOND SESSION

SEPTEMBER 20, 1994

[No. 163]

Printed for the use of the
Committee on Science, Space, and Technology

U.S. GOVERNMENT PRINTING OFFICE

87–668 CC WASHINGTON : 1995

For sale by the U.S. Government Printing Office
Superintendent of Documents, Congressional Sales Office, Washington, DC 20402
ISBN 0-16-046738-1

COMMITTEE ON SCIENCE, SPACE, AND TECHNOLOGY

GEORGE E. BROWN, Jr., California, *Chairman*

MARILYN LLOYD, Tennessee
DAN GLICKMAN, Kansas
HAROLD L. VOLKMER, Missouri
RALPH M. HALL, Texas
DAVE McCURDY, Oklahoma
TIM VALENTINE, North Carolina
ROBERT G. TORRICELLI, New Jersey
RICK BOUCHER, Virginia
JAMES A. TRAFICANT, Jr., Ohio
JAMES A. HAYES, Louisiana
JOHN S. TANNER, Tennessee
PETE GEREN, Texas
JIM BACCHUS, Florida
TIM ROEMER, Indiana
ROBERT E. (BUD) CRAMER, Jr., Alabama
DICK SWETT, New Hampshire
JAMES A. BARCIA, Michigan
HERBERT C. KLEIN, New Jersey
ERIC FINGERHUT, Ohio
PAUL McHALE, Pennsylvania
JANE HARMAN, California
DON JOHNSON, Georgia
SAM COPPERSMITH, Arizona
ANNA G. ESHOO, California
JAY INSLEE, Washington
EDDIE BERNICE JOHNSON, Texas
DAVID MINGE, Minnesota
NATHAN DEAL, Georgia
ROBERT C. SCOTT, Virginia
XAVIER BECERRA, California
PETER W. BARCA, Wisconsin
BOBBY L. RUSH, Illinois

ROBERT S. WALKER, Pennsylvania*
F. JAMES SENSENBRENNER, Jr., Wisconsin
SHERWOOD L. BOEHLERT, New York
TOM LEWIS, Florida
HARRIS W. FAWELL, Illinois
CONSTANCE A. MORELLA, Maryland
DANA ROHRABACHER, California
STEVEN H. SCHIFF, New Mexico
JOE BARTON, Texas
DICK ZIMMER, New Jersey
SAM JOHNSON, Texas
KEN CALVERT, California
MARTIN R. HOKE, Ohio
NICK SMITH, Michigan
EDWARD R. ROYCE, California
ROD GRAMS, Minnesota
JOHN LINDER, Georgia
PETER BLUTE, Massachusetts
JENNIFER DUNN, Washington
BILL BAKER, California
ROSCOE G. BARTLETT, Maryland
VERNON J. EHLERS, Michigan

ROBERT E. PALMER, *Chief of Staff*
MICHAEL RODEMEYER, *Chief Counsel*
KATHRYN HOLMES, *Administrator*
DAVID D. CLEMENT, *Republican Chief of Staff*

SUBCOMMITTEE ON SCIENCE

RICK BOUCHER, Virginia, *Chairman*

RALPH M. HALL, Texas
TIM VALENTINE, North Carolina
JAMES A. BARCIA, Michigan
DON JOHNSON, Georgia
ANNA G. ESHOO, California
E. B. JOHNSON, Texas
DAVID MINGE, Minnesota
PETER W. BARCA, Wisconsin

SHERWOOD L. BOEHLERT, New York
JOE BARTON, Texas
SAM JOHNSON, Texas
NICK SMITH, Michigan
PETER BLUTE, Massachusettes

*Ranking Republican Member.

CONTENTS

WITNESSES

THE FEDERAL FIRE PREVENTION AND CONTROL ACT AUTHORIZATION

TUESDAY, SEPTEMBER 20, 1994

HOUSE OF REPRESENTATIVES,
COMMITTEE ON SCIENCE, SPACE, AND TECHNOLOGY,
SUBCOMMITTEE ON SCIENCE,
Washington, D.C.

The subcommittee met, pursuant to call, at 9:38 a.m. in Room 2318, Rayburn House Office Building, Hon. Rick Boucher [chairman of the subcommittee] presiding.

Mr. BOUCHER. The subcommittee will come to order.

This morning the Subcommittee on Science meets to receive testimony on and then to schedule and hold a markup session on legislation to reauthorize the programs and activities under the Federal Fire Prevention and Control Act of 1974.

The 1974 Act was based largely on the recommendations of the President's National Commission on Fire Prevention and Control whose landmark report entitled "America Burning" not only identified the scope of America's fire problem, but defined an appropriate Federal role in combatting fire and its attendant devastation.

The Act established the United States Fire Administration to provide coordinated Federal support for the Nation's fire and emergency medical activities. Working closely with State and local governments, the U.S. Fire Administration fulfills this mission through public education programs, the collection and analysis of data relating to fire, the promotion of sprinkler systems and other life safety measures and research and development in fire suppression.

More recently, Congress enacted the Arson Prevention and Control Act of 1994 which establishes a coordinated Federal initiative to research the causes of arson and to strengthen existing efforts at the State and local level to combat this serious crime. The U.S. Fire Administration is administering the arson program and will soon complete the process of developing application criteria and deadlines for their submission.

The U.S. Fire Administration is also responsible for the National Fire Academy, which provides state-of-the-art training to Fire and Rescue Service personnel. Approximately 4,600 people will attend the Academy this year while an estimated 13,000 other fire fighters will receive training indirectly through the Academy's Distance Learning and Train the Trainer programs.

The print before the subcommittee this morning has two principal components. First, it reauthorizes the U.S. Fire Administration and that is through fiscal years 1997 at a level of $31.49 million for each of these three years. That sum is an amount identical to the allocation received by the Agency in the current fiscal year, in fiscal year 1994. Therefore, this sum of $31.49 million for each of the following three years represents a hard freeze in terms of the Agency's budget.

These funding levels are identical to the request submitted by the Clinton Administration and reflect the shared determination of Congress and the Executive Branch to hold the line on even the most important discretionary programs. The three-year funding freeze proposed by the Administration and contained in our legislation will pose, we believe, a serious challenge to the U.S. Fire Administrator and her staff to assure the effective allocation of resources.

To those who would challenge an even modest expenditure for fire prevention and control, I would simply point out that when the report "America Burning" was published 20 years ago, that report recommended an initial budget for the U.S. Fire Administration of some $124 million. Adjusted for inflation, that figure would be well over $300 million today and yet the Fire Administration at the present time receives only approximately one-tenth of that amount. Our authorized figures are also modest when measured against the more than $11 billion in property losses which are caused by fire in this Nation each year.

Secondly, the committee print proposes to establish for a two-year period a U.S. Fire Advisory Council. The purpose of the Council is to provide an objective outside analysis of the emergency response community of what the Fire Administration can do better to meet the goals and priorities that were set forth in "America Burning" and whether new goals and priorities are warranted, given changes in technology, fiscal resources, and other factors.

The general idea for such a council on this 20th anniversary of the landmark report was originated by the fire services community, most notably by allies to fire and energy management and has enjoyed broad support from other organizations in the community.

I am very pleased today to welcome two witnesses whose names have become synonymous with fire prevention and controlling at the Federal level. Congressman Curt Weldon from Pennsylvania is best known to this committee as the founder of the Congressional Fire Services Caucus and the Congressional Fire Services Institute. As such, he has probably done more than any other Member of Congress to focus public attention on the problem of fire in the United States and the need for a coordinated Federal response to it.

We also welcome today Carrye Brown, the U.S. Fire Administrator, who today makes her return to the House Science Committee where, for more than 12 years, she was the lead staff person dealing with fire policy, the Federal earthquake program and other matters under the committee's jurisdiction. She was a valued staff member to me and to other Members of this committee and we very much welcome her return to the committee today.

Before hearing from our two witnesses this morning, I would like to turn now to the Ranking Republican Member of our committee, the gentleman from New York, Mr. Boehlert.

Mr. BOEHLERT. Thank you very much, Mr. Chairman. Roger Allen in the Grand Rapids Press said Congress is continually appointing fact-finding committees when what we really need are fact-facing committees.

It is a fact—a tragic fact—that fire is the fourth largest accidental killer in the United States. The U.S. has the highest fire rate in the industrialized world, fire death rate. More Americans die in fires each year than in all the natural disasters combined with an average of 5,500 deaths and 30,000 civilian injuries annually.

One hundred fire fighters are killed and nearly 100,000 injured each year. Fires cost the taxpayers about $50 billion a year with direct fire property losses topping $11.2 billion.

I'm proud to say that this committee has faced facts and produced results. In May of this year, President Clinton signed into law the Arson Prevention Act, landmark legislation from the subcommittee providing States the resources required to improve arson prevention and enforcement, which complements other efforts, including the Hotel-Motel Fire Safety Act and new initiatives such as the Fire Safety Education Act. No single program is going to eliminate losses by fire, but this developing body of law and legislation are working in concert to enable our fire community to reduce enormous losses and help educate the public.

But while Congress has made great strides in recent years in preventing needless death and destruction from fire, today we have an opportunity to go yet another step forward.

Essentially, this bill would use a moderate amount of Federal money—and I'm talking about in Washington terms, petty cash—to provide leadership, coordination, and support for the Nation's fire prevention and control, fire training and education and emergency medical services activities to combat a nationwide danger that States and localities have been unable to confront alone. The Advisory Council it establishes will help accurately assess advances in technology and changes in the emergency response services and will be of great benefit to the mission of the U.S. Fire Administration.

Mr. Chairman, you have very eloquently expressed in greater detail the provisions of the legislation. I just would like to say before concluding my remarks, which I know will appear in their entirety in the record, how pleased I am to see two people before us as witnesses today that are genuine heroes.

Our kids say to us, Where are the heroes today? Curt, I don't know of anybody in the whole Congress that has more enthusiasm and more commitment to the work we are about than you do. And I can remember very vividly, as the lady sitting to your right can recall, when you came here as a freshman and had this great idea about a fire services caucus and an institute, and we listened respectfully. And as you left the room, I remember we said to ourselves, boy, this guy is a ball of fire and we'll help him, but, boy, he's got big ideas.

We didn't expect in our wildest dreams that you would succeed as well as you have, so I personally salute you. You have been a one-man band and the rest of us are all chiming in now. We are all part of this great effort, but you are the guy that really made it all happen and I am proud to be a part of it now.

And Carrye Brown, we worked so well, so close over these years together and you really are one of my heroes because I didn't know a darn thing about so much of the work of this subcommittee when I came here and you've helped to educate me, and I couldn't be prouder than I am of you to be in your very important and lofty position, and I look forward with great anticipation of performing great deeds together, all of us who are so vitally interested in doing a better job for the American people.

So with that, Mr. Chairman, let me say we have got a couple of heroes before us as witnesses. We don't often have that and I am looking forward to hearing everything they say.

[The prepared statement of Mr. Boehlert follows:]

CONGRESSMAN SHERWOOD BOEHLERT (R-NY)
SEPTEMBER 20, 1994
STATEMENT ON "THE FIRE ADMINISTRATION AUTHORIZATION ACT OF 1994"

THANK YOU, MR. CHAIRMAN. ROGER ALLEN IN THE GRAND RAPIDS *PRESS* SAID, "CONGRESS IS CONTINUALLY APPOINTING FACT-FINDING COMMITTEES, WHEN WHAT WE REALLY NEED ARE SOME FACT-FACING COMMITTEES."

IT IS A FACT -- A TRAGIC FACT -- THAT FIRE IS THE FOURTH LARGEST ACCIDENTAL KILLER IN THE UNITED STATES. THE U.S. HAS THE HIGHEST FIRE DEATH RATE IN THE INDUSTRIALIZED WORLD. MORE AMERICANS DIE IN FIRES EACH YEAR THAN IN ALL NATURAL DISASTERS COMBINED, WITH AN AVERAGE OF 5,500 DEATHS AND 30,000 CIVILIAN INJURIES ANNUALLY. ONE-HUNDRED FIREFIGHTERS ARE KILLED AND NEARLY 100,000 INJURED EACH YEAR. FIRES COST THE TAXPAYERS ABOUT $50 BILLION A YEAR, WITH DIRECT FIRE PROPERTY LOSSES TOPPING $11.2 BILLION.

I AM PROUD TO SAY THAT THIS COMMITTEE HAS FACED FACTS AND PRODUCED RESULTS. IN MAY OF THIS YEAR, PRESIDENT CLINTON SIGNED INTO LAW THE ARSON PREVENTION ACT -- LANDMARK LEGISLATION FROM THIS SUBCOMMITTEE PROVIDING STATES THE RESOURCES REQUIRED TO IMPROVE ARSON PREVENTION AND ENFORCEMENT. THIS COMPLIMENTS OTHER EFFORTS, INCLUDING: THE HOTEL AND MOTEL SAFETY ACT AND NEW INITIATIVES SUCH AS THE FIRE SAFETY EDUCATION ACT. NO SINGLE PROGRAM IS GOING TO ELIMINATE LOSSES BY FIRE, BUT THIS DEVELOPING BODY OF LAW AND LEGISLATION ARE WORKING IN CONCERT TO ENABLE OUR FIRE COMMUNITY TO REDUCE ENORMOUS LOSSES AND HELP EDUCATE THE PUBLIC.

BUT WHILE CONGRESS HAS MADE GREAT STRIDES IN RECENT YEARS IN PREVENTING NEEDLESS DEATH AND DESTRUCTION FROM FIRE, TODAY WE HAVE AN OPPORTUNITY TO GO YET ANOTHER STEP.

ESSENTIALLY, THIS BILL WOULD USE A MODERATE AMOUNT OF FEDERAL MONEY TO PROVIDE LEADERSHIP, COORDINATION AND SUPPORT FOR THE NATION'S FIRE PREVENTION AND CONTROL, FIRE TRAINING AND EDUCATION AND EMERGENCY MEDICAL SERVICES ACTIVITIES -- TO COMBAT A NATIONWIDE DANGER THAT STATES AND LOCALITIES HAVE BEEN UNABLE TO CONFRONT ALONE. THE ADVISORY COUNCIL IT ESTABLISHES WILL HELP ACCURATELY ASSESS ADVANCES IN TECHNOLOGY AND CHANGES IN THE EMERGENCY RESPONSE SERVICES AND WILL BE OF GREAT BENEFIT TO THE MISSION OF THE U.S. FIRE ADMINISTRATION.

I WANT TO THANK CHAIRMAN BOUCHER -- WHO SHARES MY CONVICTION FOR THIS BILL -- FOR CONVENING THIS HEARING AND MARK-UP TODAY. I ALSO LOOK FORWARD TO THE TESTIMONY OF A REAL LEADER ON ISSUES AFFECTING THE EMERGENCY SERVICES COMMUNITY, MY DISTINGUISHED COLLEAGUE CURT WELDON, WHO IS THE FOUNDER OF THE

CONGRESSIONAL FIRE CAUCUS. I WOULD ALSO LIKE TO WELCOME U.S. FIRE ADMINISTRATOR CARRYE BROWN IN HER FIRST APPEARANCE BEFORE THE SCIENCE COMMITTEE, ALTHOUGH SHE IS NO STRANGER HERE AFTER SPENDING MORE THAN TWELVE YEARS AS A PROFESSIONAL STAFF MEMBER ON THIS SUBCOMMITTEE.

THE PROGRAM WE ARE TALKING ABOUT TODAY IS NEAR AND DEAR TO MY HEART. I AM VERY PLEASED WITH THE PRIORITIES THAT ARE INCLUDED IN THIS DRAFT BILL; I WILL NOT ENUMERATE THEM AT THIS TIME, BUT SIMPLY REITERATE THAT THIS MODEST INCREASE IS INDEED NEEDED FOR THE FIRE ADMINISTRATION TO CARRY OUT ITS MANY ESSENTIAL PROGRAMS. THE SUCCESS OF THE U.S. FIRE ADMINISTRATION IS OBVIOUS IN THE DRAMATIC DECREASE IN FIRE-RELATED DEATHS OVER THE PAST TWO DECADES -- FROM APPROXIMATELY 12,000 ANNUALLY TO LESS THAN 5,500 ANNUALLY. FACING FACTS IS MAKING A DIFFERENCE.

Mr. BOUCHER. Thank you very much, Mr. Boehlert, for those remarks and also for the excellent work you've provided over the years in helping to fashion a Federal response to the problem of fire in America. You have also been a real leader in this effort and, as Chairman of this subcommittee, I very much value the contributions you make.

The gentleman from California, Mr. Brown.

Mr. BROWN OF CALIFORNIA. Thank you, Mr. Chairman.

It is a great pleasure for me also to be here this morning to welcome these two distinguished witnesses, both of whom have contributed in the Congress and in this committee to the establishment of the effective fire programs that we have today.

I would like to expand on that, but I think you and Mr. Boehlert have both reflected my views in the statements that you've made.

Let me just add this point as a challenge to the committee and perhaps to our two witnesses also. I am not happy with the fiscal situation that confronts the Nation today and the need to propound an authorization bill which is, as the Chairman indicated, a hard freeze for the next three years. I don't think that that reflects the kind of vision that we had 20 years ago about the needs to be more effective in terms of reducing the losses from fire and other catastrophes. I might say that was reflected in the report "America Burning".

It may be that today is the time to consider the need for another review of what we have been doing in connection with fire programs and to look with a new sense of creativity about how we might enhance these programs through some of the popular approaches that are being taken today. I refer to the terms of government-industry partnership and Reinventing Government which have become so popular.

There is, it seems to me, the possibility that we could develop a more effective partnership between the Federal Government's role in fire prevention, the local governments and State governments which bear the great burden—the great majority of the burden of fire prevention services, and the insurance industry which of course bears the great portion of the losses of fire through the insurance programs that are in effect.

I am sure that there is today excellent cooperation between these three components. I think we should look at the situation, however, to see if we couldn't perhaps come up with some ideas that would improve that cooperation and to reprioritize the various activities going on all with the same aim at educating the American public to the hazards of fire and creating a more effective institutional force for both fire prevention and for education and the importance of citizen participation in fire.

I raise this as a challenge which I would like to have our distinguished witnesses consider, I'd like to have this committee consider. If in fact this time is ripe in the light of the hard freeze budget that we have to reexamine the opportunities that might exist, then I would like to see this committee initiate the steps to review these possibilities and start us toward a new generation of more effective activity with regard to fire.

I'm not sure that I've given sufficient thought to this. I will depend upon the committee itself and the subcommittee Chairman to give it a reality check, but I offer that as a suggestion this morning, Mr. Chairman. And thank you for this opportunity.

Mr. BOUCHER. Thank you very much, Mr. Chairman. We will certainly counsel with you on that recommendation which strikes me as an excellent one and we will try to develop it thoroughly in the time to come.

The Chair would ask if the gentlelady from Texas, Ms. Johnson, has an opening statement?

Ms. JOHNSON OF TEXAS. No, Mr. Chairman.

Mr. BOUCHER. Mr. Weldon, we would be pleased to hear from you this morning. Without objection, your prepared statement will be made a part of the record and we welcome your summary.

STATEMENT OF HON. CURT WELDON, A REPRESENTATIVE IN CONGRESS FROM THE STATE OF PENNSYLVANIA

Mr. WELDON. Thank you, Mr. Chairman. It is a very high honor for me to appear before this subcommittee, especially in light of the leadership that you have provided personally and the support and leadership of Mr. Boehlert.

You know, this committee, under the chairmanship of our good friend from California and the Ranking Member from Pennsylvania, was supportive of the Fire Service of this country during the early and mid-1980s when, unfortunately, the Administration of my party was not as supportive as it could have and should have been, and under the leaders who during that vacuum were there to support these men and women with the kinds of priorities at the Federal level that they needed to have addressed, and everyone is aware of that and appreciates the work that you did.

Since I've been here over the past eight years, our goal has been to basically attempt to raise the awareness of this group of brave Americans to a new level at both the State and Federal level to assist in some of the priorities that they have.

Elevating this young lady to my right to the position of Fire Administrator was a very positive move by the Clinton Administration earlier this year to help continue the awareness raising that has occurred over the past 10 years or so.

Let me start off by relating two stories that I think perhaps—or perhaps three stories that relate—where we've come and the kind of attitude changes occurring in America.

On Friday, I had the occasion to visit the neighboring State of Delaware where I was asked to make a few remarks to the Delaware State Fire Fighters Convention. I entered the room and there were probably 700 people there. I went up to the podium and there on the podium was the Governor of Delaware, Tom Carper; Senator Joe Biden; Senator Bill Roth; and the only Member of Congress from Delaware, Mike Castle, as well as every major statewide elected official in that State.

The Delaware Fire Service is an example of what's happening across America and I think Joe Biden's words sum it up the best. "In Delaware, there are three political parties: There are the Republicans, and the Democrats, and the Fire Service. And their power is not necessarily in that order". And the respect that they now have in that State from both political parties and the leadership of both parties is an example of what's happening across the country.

Earlier this year—in fact it was in early September—the first Statewide debate between the two candidates for Governor of Pennsylvania, Tom Ridge and Mark Singel, was hosted by the State Fire Service and a new institute they formed in Pennsylvania. The moderator was none other than Hal Bruno, the ABC News Political Director who hosted one of the debates for the Presidential race several years ago. As you know, Hal also happens to be a volunteer fire fighter in one of our suburban D.C. counties. That was the first and, until this time, only debate among the two major candidates for governor in the State of Pennsylvania.

Earlier this year, I was down in Alabama for the third time with 2,000 people in their Convention Center in the heart of their downtown area with the Governor and two-thirds of their State legislature, as the candidates running for the governor's position and the various offices all came together to show their support of the Fire Service of that State.

And in fact across America what I refer to as the sleeping giant has awakened and now public officials are paying attention. Much like you all paid attention during the 1980s when it was not necessarily the popular thing to do politically, that same attitude now is becoming pervasive across this country.

It is important because of the one-and-a-half million men and women who serve in the Fire Service of this country, most of them volunteer also but about 200,000 paid fire fighters in our cities and larger community. They don't necessarily want bigger government. In many cases, they simply want the government not to impose regulations they can't comply with or things that they in fact can't deal with.

They want to be respected. They want to be acknowledged. They want to have a U.S. Fire Administration that understands who they are and what they are all about. They want to have a national training system that helps train their trainers as the U.S. Fire Academy has done so well and is doing so well under Carrye's leadership. And they want to have a recognition that they are the first responders in America to all disasters.

Sometimes in this country we apply a misnomer to the Fire Service. They think they are the men and women who sit on the back of fire trucks or who in fact only deal with the large fires in the country. They really are much more than that. Every major disaster this country has faced, the first responders are the men and women that you all are working with. Whether it is the DC-10 crash in Sioux City, Iowa or whether it is the wildlands fires in Yellowstone or Southern California, Loma Prieta Earthquake, Hurricane Andrew, the World Trade Center disaster, or whether it is a two-story house fire in Sherry's district in New York or a grass fire in your district, Mr. Boucher. Every one of those incidents, the first responders are the people that you are working on behalf of.

They—even more than our military, our civil defense—are the people who form the backbone of our emergency response network. And the work that you do here, while it may appear small from a dollar standpoint, is dramatic because it is the basic help from the

Federal Government for them to be able to meet the objectives in their own local community.

As you know, there are 32,000 of these organizations across America. They are the heart and soul of their communities. They organize the parades and festivities. They're so much more than just the people who put out the fires. They are the people who keep America strong, not just from the standpoint of disasters, but they keep the social fabric of our small towns strong.

You all know, you have volunteer fire departments in your communities. They are the heart and soul of the community where all the activities center, that organizes the events, raises money for the families burned out of their houses, or people who are in need, host the boy scout troop, and oftentimes is the place where elections are held.

Mr. BOEHLERT. Don't forget softball. And, boy, if we don't—that is right, the softball leagues and teams that are provided and just the general positive feelings in our communities. At the Federal level, we've got to acknowledge that and we've got to provide the support to these people to continue to do the job they're doing.

In the inner cities, the paid fire fighters who face the most serious occupation in the world under terrible circumstances, they need our help with our cities facing their budget dilemmas. They need for us to understand them.

In our suburbs, the volunteers need to know that we are there, not just to support them, but to keep the government out of their hair and let people do their job. Let us support them but not impose mandates without the dollars not to do things, and we end up not really helping them but in the end we are actually hurting them.

That's the message of the Fire Service of this country. They appreciate with every ounce of energy in their bodies the work that you all have done and they know the job that you've done, whether it is the Hotel-Motel Fire Safety Act which, for the first time, says that smoke detectors are important, and detection systems are important, and the use of building construction considerations in life safety in our hotels, whether it is legislation dealing with fire education which you have been in the forefront of.

The arson bill is a major landmark piece of legislation, even though it is a very small amount of money, $2.5 million. It sends a signal that we care about the problem of arson and the terrible damage that it is causing all around and the loss of life. Fire fighters are people who are killed by deliberately set fires, not even counting the amount of damage and destruction that is caused in communities, and the hurt to our insurance industry which all of us have to pay for.

So I am here to applaud you for that work and say, please keep it up. The Fire Service is awake now, it is alert politically. Our annual dinner, which you have all attended, we've had six of them. We average about 2,000 people each spring at that dinner. This past year, President Clinton was our key note speaker. Last year it was Vice President Al Gore.

In six years—and there aren't many groups that can say that they had the Vice President and President who are Democrats and the President and Vice President who are Republicans. We had

Ron Howard and the cast of Backdraft and Charlton Heston and everyone you can think of involved with disasters in this country. We have reached a new level of awareness.

We can't solve all of their problems. The fact that you are listening is the most important thing. The fact that you are willing to listen to what they have to say and remember fundamentally that they are the first responders to disasters in this country. Our Congressional Disaster Task Force, which is being chaired right now by Dick Durbin and Bill Emerson, will come out with a series of recommendations. Many of them will apply to how they fund disasters.

There will be some peripheral recommendations dealing with the issues of fires. Some of them will be right in line with the remarks of the Chairman of the full committee in regard to looking to how we're responding to the original "America Burning" report that was issued some 20 years ago. Your suggestion in the authorization bill to have an advisory council is outstanding. It is right on the mark because the Fire Service will have a formal way of advising in terms of their priorities as it relates to the original "America Burning" report.

I applaud that totally. I think that's a great idea. In addition, I guess I would say my only major concern, as has been outlined I think by each of you, is the hard freeze on the funding level. Since 1989, we in fact have been able to raise slightly the amount of authorization each year for these important programs. This hard freeze is going to be difficult only because you know the people we are helping are volunteers, for the most part. And boy, what a tremendous return we get for our dollars, a very small amount of dollars, for all these millions of hours of volunteer service that take place across the country.

So that would be my only hesitation. But I understand the constraints that you are operating in and I support you in that fight to keep the funding level where it is now and not have any reductions occur.

But in closing, I say thank you to each of you. Thank you to the Chairman and Ranking Member of the full committee, Mr. Brown, and Mr. Walker who have been supportive of everything we've asked for, and the two of you for your leadership. And Carrye Brown, all I can say is I'm one of her biggest cheerleaders, and while I can't stay to hear her testimony, I know it will be as solid as is her leadership, and we are all behind her while they continue to fight the battle for the men and women who protect our communities.

Thank you.

[The prepared statement of Mr. Weldon follows:]

87-668 O - 95 - 2

TESTIMONY OF HON. CURT WELDON

HOUSE COMMITTEE ON SCIENCE, SPACE, AND TECHNOLOGY

ON THE REAUTHORIZATION OF THE U.S. FIRE ADMINISTRATION

Chairman Boucher, Ranking Member Boucher, and Members of the Subcommittee. Thank you for permitting me to testify before you this morning. I appreciate having the opportunity to work with this panel on furthering a goal which we all share: preventing the loss of life and destruction of property from fire.

It has now been nearly eight years since I was elected to this body, and in that time I have seen tremendous improvements in Congress' efforts to reduce the costs of fire in this country. The Congressional Fire Services Caucus, under the strong leadership of our good friend Steny Hoyer, continues to advance legislation which will save untold lives and protect those fire fighters who risk their lives to save us.

I also would like to praise this Subcommittee and its distinguished members, notably Chairman Boucher and Ranking Member Boehlert. This panel has been receptive toward legislation pushed by the national fire service and has devised its own agenda to contribute to the life safety of all Americans.

On behalf of the nation's first responders, let me again thank you for all of your work on this critical issue. Today, I have brought some of those dedicated professionals with me. Seated in the audience are eleven fire fighters from Maryland. Among these faculty members from the Maryland Fire and Rescue Institute are Director Steve Edwards and former Director John Hoagland. Also present today are two CPR trainers from Montgomery County, Maryland. One of them is Mary Beth Michos, who is also the Emergency Medical Services Section Chair for the International Association of Fire Chiefs.

I am here today to support this Subcommittee's efforts to reauthorize the United States Fire Administration. As the Founder of the Congressional Fire Services Caucus and a former fire chief, I know the importance of the work done by the United States Fire Administration. As an educator of the public and the fire service, the USFA fills an important role in the public safety of every citizen of this country.

We are all familiar with the outstanding leadership which Carrye Brown has brought to the USFA. Although I think Congress misses her outstanding work on this panel, the American people have been well-served by President Clinton' selection of Ms. Brown to head the USFA.

The accomplishments of the USFA are truly outstanding and bear repeating here today. In 1993, the National Fire Academy granted certificates to 3,350 students at the Maryland center. Moreover, another 6,400 students in 48 states received off-campus training. Another 3,369 firefighters, mostly volunteers from 26 states, attended weekend training at the Academy.

The USFA also provided a great deal of education directly t the American public. The Administration's home fire safety program reached more than 250,000 homes by the distribution of safety checklists. Over 100,000 Head Start classes received USI fire safety kits. And USFA fire safety training packets were used to instruct 76,000 fire and EMS personnel.

Mr. Chairman, these important programs cost money. But the are also critical. Congress has continued to fund the USFA because its work saves lives and property everyday. It is my hope that this Committee will continue its commitment to the extraordinary work of the USFA in the years to come. It is with some regret, therefore, that I express my support for the Chairman's mark of the USFA authorization. Since 1989, Congress has continually increased funding for the Fire Administration. The proposed budget authorization for the Administration over th next three years would be held constant at just under $31.5 million.

Mr. Chairman, I think we all recognize that this level of funding will prevent the USFA from developing and implementing all of the life saving educational programs which they might otherwise undertake. All of us involved in the effort to reduce the toll which fire and other disasters take on America each year would like to see the budget of the Fire Administration increased further so that they might expand the fire safety education programs already in place. However, in this time of fiscal responsibility, I recognize the Committee's desire to hold down the growth in all federal programs. I hope that this Subcommittee, and all of our colleagues in Congress, will be responsive to the future financial and legislative requirements of the USFA.

Finally, Mr. Chairman, let me address one other important issue. Twenty years ago, Congress established the National Commission on Fire Prevention and Control. That panel produced a report, known as "America Burning" which was a landmark document. "America Burning" was a comprehensive look at the fire problem in this country and laid out a strategy for reducing the loss of life and property from fires. That report continues to provide important insights for the fire and life safety community.

In an effort to update the work of the National Commission, Chairman Boucher has proposed a U.S. Fire Advisory Council. I strongly support this plan and heartily congratulate the Chairman for his innovative vision. While the financial resources to re-create the 1974 Commission may not exist today, the Fire Advisory Council will aid the Fire Administration in its continuing educational efforts. It is my hope that the panel, slated to include twelve individuals, will be directed to make concrete recommendations to the USFA and the Congress on ways to further improve this outstanding agency.

Mr. Chairman and members of the Subcommittee, thank you again for the opportunity to appear before this panel today. I look forward to working with this Committee on other issues of fire and life safety in the years to come.

Mr. BOUCHER. Curt, thank you very much for that excellent statement and the leadership you are helping to provide as we fashion a Federal response to the problem of fire in America.

Before you leave, let me just ask if any Member of the committee has a question or comment in response to your testimony.

Mr. BROWN OF CALIFORNIA. I have a comment, Mr. Chairman.

Mr. BOUCHER. Mr. Brown.

Mr. BROWN OF CALIFORNIA. Let me say that I was inspired by the vision that you have of the importance of the Fire Service and, under most circumstances, when someone comes before us to espouse the great value of an organization and so on, I discount it considerably because of obvious biases.

And in this case, I think that we have consistently underestimated the value of that large core of people who are engaged in providing basic safety services to our communities. You have illustrated some of the many ways in which they build the fabric of the community as well as helping to alleviate disasters and other tragedies.

What this country needs today more than anything else is strong fabric that bind together our communities and create a base on which we can develop a healthy and positive sense of the importance of our community life.

I would urge you to use your role and, in the Fire Caucus, to try and build on that and to develop a conceptualization of the broader role that the Fire Service plays as a part of our united efforts to strengthen the communities that all over America seem to be deteriorating today for a number of different reasons. We need to use every resource, and this may be one of the most important resources that we have.

Mr. WELDON. If I might respond just briefly then, Mr. Chairman, if that would be appropriate. I agree totally with the sentiments of the full committee chairman and with the current leadership of our caucus, Chairman Steny Hoyer, who's a good friend to all of us and who is doing a fantastic job.

We have tried to carry that message across America. It is kind of there but you don't realize it's there. I mean, in 32,000 communities in America, from New York City to the smallest town in your home State of California, there are groups of people who get together to do public service, in those cases as volunteers, and who even go out and raise the money for the trucks and equipment and then on top of that support the community in so many other ways.

That really is the message of what the Fire Service is all about and that's a very important thing for us to keep reinforcing. They are not just the people who handle fires and disasters. They really are the heart and soul of our community. I mean, if you want to look at a group that does more to keep our towns together, you can't find any group that is as well organized and as aggressive as the men and women of the Nation's Fire Service. I mean, in every town in America they are there, they are the social hub, the recreational hall or the fire halls where the young couple holds the wedding reception. It's where you vote on Election Day in many cases.

They are the first one you call to organize a search party. They get the cats out of the trees. They pump the basements when they are flooded. They organize the parades, the Memorial Day celebrations. They organize the softball leagues. They organize everything that makes a town great and they are involved in all this.

And frequently this is all overlooked. The men and women who start out in the Fire Service are the ones who oftentimes become the local mayors and town council members. And they are Republicans and Democrats. We have got as many Democrats—probably more Democrats—in the Fire Service than Republicans. That's important because they really do form the fabric of community.

So if there is any one thing we should be doing down here is trying to help those people, keeping them involved. Where we can't get the volunteers especially in our cities, we have got to come forward and support the paid fire fighters because they have a greater challenge because there are less of them, and in the big cities there are more hazards and more difficulties.

You are right, Mr. Chairman, we need to take you on a national road tour. And if you want to go out and speak to all these groups, I will make arrangements.

Mr. BROWN OF CALIFORNIA. May I respond just very briefly to that. I do talk to a lot of the fire services quite frequently and they have been the backbone of my political support over the last 40 years as a matter of fact.

I want to add one additional thing which comes to mind as a result of my experience with the local fire agencies in California. They are effective carriers of international cooperation in our area. There's hardly a Fire Department in Southern California that doesn't have a relationship with some Mexican or other foreign Fire Service, frequently contributing used fire equipment, other things of that sort.

And they have built on the relationship that frequently is part of our sister cities or relationships of that type and have become essential bonds in uniting the fire services across national boundaries, and I think this is a very important element that needs to be included.

Mr. WELDON. And I don't want to continue to dominate, but I have to just follow up. Today in Sarajevo, with all the troubles in that country, John Jordan, a volunteer fire fighter from Rhode Island, has put together the emergency response system in that city. He started two years ago when no one else was there. When the fire chief from Sarajevo who came to our country, Keenan Slinich, to speak at our dinner last year was assassinated, there was no one else there. John Jordan, a volunteer from our country, went over there and established it.

Fire communities from throughout this country, most of them volunteer, sent three airplanes filled with four fire trucks, ladders, hoses, and equipment that they donated to Sarajevo. And currently, John Jordan is recognized by the U.N. command as the emergency response leader for that city. Volunteers from this country are going over on tours of one month at a time volunteering to serve the people of that city, whether they are Serbs, Croats, Muslims or whatever in terms of their emergency response needs.

So Mr. Chairman, you are again right on the mark. There are examples like that all around the world where the American Fire

Service is giving of itself and asking for nothing in return except to be told that they have done a job well.

Thank you, and I will now leave.

Mr. BOUCHER. Thank you very much, Mr. Weldon. We appreciate your appearance here, and your leadership. And if we encounter any difficulties with the legislation, we are going to be calling on you and the Members of the Fire Services Caucus to help us out.

Mr. WELDON. Thank you.

Mr. BOEHLERT. Mr. Chairman, I just wish Mr. Weldon would be a little more enthusiastic about the subject.

Mr. BOUCHER. Mrs. Brown, we will be happy to hear from you. Your prepared statement will be made a part of the record and we would welcome your oral summary.

STATEMENT OF HON. CARRYE B. BROWN, ADMINISTRATOR, UNITED STATES FIRE ADMINISTRATION, FEDERAL EMERGENCY MANAGEMENT AGENCY

Mrs. CARRYE BROWN. Good morning, Chairman Boucher, Ranking Member Boehlert, full committee Chairman Brown and Congresswoman Eddie Bernice Johnson. I am very honored to testify before you today on legislation to reauthorize the Federal Fire Prevention and Control Act.

I am especially honored to testify before you because your committee has been the leader in crafting fire safety legislation to make America a safer place. I know that.

For more than a decade as a staffer, I've had the pleasure of looking at the House from the outside, now I'm on the inside. And what I take to that job are values that I've learned from you, demonstrated values.

As a fire administrator, my greatest challenge is to put limited resources to work where they will make the greatest difference in saving lives and reducing losses. What does that mean? That means looking at all—and I do mean all—of our programs and seeing if we are meeting the needs of our customers.

And who are our customers? I've learned from you that, first, our customer is the American public who are the potential victims of fire, and second, our customers are the Fire Service community, the ones who are called to cope with our failures in fire.

It means that I need to go back to our roots in grounding the USFA's programs and all of its activities in the basics. Those basics are grounded for me in "America Burning", the definitive report on this Nation's fire problem that laid out recommendations that are still valid today.

Twenty years ago, as you said, Mr. Boucher, Congress followed one of those recommendations and created the USFA to be the Federal focus point on fire safety. I've read it and reread that original Public Law that we are reauthorizing today and I must say it still makes very good sense. As Fire Administrator, I have decided to go back to the four basic areas as identified by Congress when they passed the enabling Act to create the USFA.

Those four basic areas are: Public education and awareness, fire data collection and analysis, Fire Service training, and fire technology and research.

Today, I would like to share with you some of the priorities I plan to pursue over the next three years. As I've said before, for each and every program, I am going to be asking and I'm already asking what is the taxpayer getting? Will this program save lives or reduce losses?

I promise you that each program regardless of its history, regardless of its constituency, must pass these tests. With that promise clearly stated, let me share my blueprint for a safer America. As I said, I have outlined four issues. I am not going to elaborate because I think I will do that in questions, but I will target one.

The first is we need to do more in public education. Without a doubt, the Fire Administration must provide fire safety and EMS programs that help make citizens and communities safer. Over the past years, the USFA has developed some great education programs. However, in these days of dwindling resources, I think the USFA must provide targeted efforts to reach those most at risk from fire. Those are our young, our senior citizens, our disabled and our economically disadvantaged.

Let me give an example—a couple of examples. This summer, the USFA launched the largest effort to date to reach the Spanish speaking audience with fire safety information but we weren't the only people involved. More than 2,000 chapters of American Red Cross are a part of this effort along with the National SAFE KIDS Campaign with its chapters nationwide. These two groups have worked with us from the beginning to create and distribute bilingual fire safety materials. The demand for the materials has been overwhelming.

In addition, we are very proud of the Advertising Council because the council has selected fire safety for young children as a major initiative for the next three years. Working with the USFA, the council is developing its first public national ad council campaign along with materials for use at the local level. With an equivalent donated value of about $30 million for advertising, the impact on fire safety will be tremendous.

And then just to elaborate a little further on public education and what it can do, I went down to New Orleans this summer to speak before the International Association on Black Professional Fire Fighters, and I had an opportunity while I was down there to participate in a smoke detector installation campaign. It was coming on the heels of a very tragic fire down there. Several children lost their lives in the fire.

And what was gratifying to me and demonstrated to me the need and the power of public education is the fact that Miss Mary, an 80-year-old lady, allowed the Fire Service organizations down there to come in and install a smoke detector in her home. And her message to the public—because she did speak to the public on television—was that this is something that we need to do. She understood. That campaign was able to reach her and others.

My second priority is to fire data collection and analysis.

The third priority will be the National Fire Academy, making programs relevant and accessible to all Fire Service personnel regardless of where they work.

The final priority is technology and research. After more than 17 years with the Committee on Science, Space, and Technology, I recognize the vital importance that technology and scientific research bring to reducing fire losses. One of my first efforts was to bring a Chief Scientist into the USFA in recognition of the importance of scientific research and technology to fulfilling the goals of the "America Burning" Report.

I'm going to skip a lot of this because I recognize, as a staffer, the importance of being brief and getting to the point.

Mr. Chairman, this concludes my priorities for the USFA. We would like to thank you for sponsoring the Administration's proposal for reauthorizing the Fire Administration as contained in Section 2 of your bill.

Now I'm going to do something that I have not had the pleasure of doing before. I'm going to have to tell you that the USFA opposes the establishment of this Council, the Advisory Council that is in Section 3 of the bill, because it would duplicate existing efforts and require funding to the detriment of needed programs elsewhere.

Quite frankly, we believe that we receive substantial input from the Fire Service community on a regular basis. However, I want you to know that I look forward to working with you on this to address concerns that the Fire Service and the committee might have regarding this.

Mr. Chairman, and Members, as I provided staff support for the Hotel-Motel Fire Safety Act, the Arson Prevention Act, legislation dealing with the authorization of the USFA and also about a decade ago, I listened to Mr. Brown and saw him put in language that addressed an "all hazards" approach to the earthquake hazards reduction program and the emergency management efforts which are now embraced by our current Director of FEMA. I saw the commitment and leadership shown by all of you. It is now my turn to implement these visions and to provide the same commitment and leadership to reduce the loss of life and property due to fires in the U.S.

Thank you, Mr. Chairman, for the opportunity to appear before this subcommittee. I would be pleased to answer any questions you and other Members of the committee might have.

[The prepared statement of Mrs. Carrye Brown follows:]

Statement of
The Honorable Carrye B. Brown
Administrator
United States Fire Administration
Federal Emergency Management Agency
Before
The Science Subcommittee
Committee on Science, Space, and Technology
United States House of Representatives
September 20, 1994

Good morning, Chairman Boucher, Ranking Member Boehlert and Members of the Subcommittee, I am Carrye B. Brown, Administrator of the United States Fire Administration (USFA) in the Federal Emergency Management Agency (FEMA). I am pleased to have the opportunity to testify on USFA programs. This morning I will discuss the planned activities and priorities for Fiscal Years 1995 through 1997.

Fire continues to be a serious national problem. Although, deaths from fire have decreased significantly over the past two decades, the United States still has one of the highest fire death rates per capita in the industrialized world. Ongoing and past USFA efforts, among them the very successful smoke detector and public awareness programs, have helped to reduce the Nation's deaths to some 5,700 annually. However, we still continue to lose billions of dollars in our National economy to fires each year.

USFA has provided, with strong Administration, Congressional and constituent support, a very significant Federal focus on the Nation's fire problem. It serves as facilitator and catalyst, helping the fire service community act as one to develop the most efficient and effective programs and response strategies.

It functions as a conduit and clearinghouse, heightening fire safety awareness and providing public education materials to assist the fire service community.

None of these efforts would succeed without the support of the Nation's fire service community and without the talent and commitment they provide to USFA.

How can we reach our goal of achieving a fire safe America? When will it happen? The answers lie in public awareness of the fire problem and, most importantly, in our citizens' acceptance of their responsibility for the solution. The under use of the single greatest resource in fire prevention efforts, the public themselves, must be aggressively pursued for expanded involvement and commitment to fire safety.

I would like to highlight for the Subcommittee the areas that USFA will focus on during the next three years. They include public education and fire safety; fire technology research and firefighter health and safety programs; fire data collection and analysis and fire training programs.

Public Education and Fire Safety Programs

Recently, USFA joined the Consumer Product Safety Commission in a demonstration project addressing repair of electrical wiring problems in older homes. The outcome of this project will be used to promote the repair of electrical systems in these older homes where a significant number of middle and low-income people live. The highest risk groups, those most vulnerable to the threat of fire, are the young and the elderly.

The USFA has launched the largest effort to date to reach Spanish speaking audiences with fire safety information. But we aren't the only people involved. More than 2,000 chapters of the American Red Cross are part of this effort along with the National SAFE KIDS Campaign with its chapters nationwide. These two groups have worked with us from the beginning to create and distribute bilingual fire safety materials.

In addition, the Advertising Council has selected fire safety for young children as a major initiative for the next three years. Working with the Fire Administration, the Council is developing a public national ad campaign along with materials for use at the local level. With an equivalent donated value of $30 million dollars of advertising, the impact on fire safety will be tremendous.

Other program efforts for the next three years include:

- Continuing to develop and disseminate specialized information for State agencies and local fire service with special focus on groups who are particularly vulnerable to fire such as children, the elderly, minorities, physically impaired and Native Americans.
- Enhancing National public educational awareness campaigns with special emphasis on high-risk populations through focus on fire safety, smoke detector installation and maintenance.
- Continuing the annual National ceremony to honor firefighters who have given their lives in service to their communities.

Fire Research & Firefighter Health and Safety

USFA continues to encourage private sector participation in local and State fire prevention programs and to gain private sector support for the USFA's research and development projects. The level of support gained to date is evident in programs such as public education and awareness, new technology development and testing, and demonstration projects. Because firefighters are still confronted with unanswered questions concerning the ability of their protective clothing to adequately protect them from fire, USFA has funded a special study which will analyze the thermal protective property of firefighter protective clothing.

Additional program efforts include:

- Expanding efforts with building and fire code organizations to address evolving technology and fire protection challenges and continue to encourage fire service participation in the National consensus codes process.
- Continuing work on the development and dissemination of improved hazardous materials response information to assist first responders deal more effectively and safely with hazardous materials emergencies.
- Continuing research into new technologies for vehicle extrication.

- Continuing research into new technologies for technical rescue and other programs to support local-level technical rescue operations, such as: confined ~~confirmed~~ space rescue, building collapse (urban) search and rescue, trench rescue, rope/high angle rescue, water rescue, and other special rescue situations.
- Identifying and sponsoring research on the application of sprinkler systems for residential structures, data processing facilities, and other special occupancies.
- Conducting special studies and analyses for firefighter protective clothing and equipment for structural firefighting.

<u>Fire Data Collection and Analysis</u>

Program efforts in this area will include:

- Continuing operation of the current National Fire Incident Reporting System program in conjunction with National Fire Information Council to improve data collection and analysis capabilities.
- Continuing work on the identification of causes of firefighter serious injuries and fatalities.
- Continuing the USFA Technical Report Series with a focus on major fire loss incidents, firefighter injuries/fatalities, and code related fire problems.

<u>Training Programs</u>

These program efforts through our National Fire Academy include:

- Offering technical assistance to state and local communities in the form of train-the-trainer concepts; forming partnerships with public service organizations and continuing to identify and promote successful local-community prevention programs.
- Developing or revising resident, field and/or regional delivery courses; conducting evaluation of individual courses and evaluation of Academy curriculum impact; continuing a National needs assessment for Academy curriculum planning; expanding use of computer-based learning; and providing American Council on Education accreditation review and listing of all new and revised courses.
- Identifying new opportunities to enhance volunteer fire service roles and efforts; continuing coordination efforts with other Federal and State Agencies and public interest organizations on fire related matters; and expanding development efforts for fire service involvement in public/private partnerships.

Another area of interest to the Subcommittee is PL 103-254, the Arson Prevention Act of 1994. Within one week of the President's May 19 signing of the legislation into law, I became U.S. Fire Administrator charged with the responsibility of implementing the provisions of the law.

87-668 O - 95 - 3

The first task was to issue a rule to implement the provisions of the section on "Arson Prevention Grants." I am pleased to report to the Subcommittee, that we plan to publish a proposed rule in the Federal Register this week. After a 45 day-period for public comments, a final rule will be revised as needed, published and implemented.

The proposed rule contains the necessary provisions from the public law, including the 10 grant goals, state qualifications criteria, technical assistance and consultation and cooperation. The proposed rule also contains grant application procedures and competitive evaluation criteria.

Mr. Chairman, we would like to thank you for sponsoring the Administration's proposal for reauthorization of the Fire Administration as contained in Section 2 of your bill. Mr. Chairman, USFA would also like to comment on Section 3 of the reauthorization bill that would establish the United States Fire Advisory Council. USFA opposes the establishment of a statutorily based council--consistent with the President's guidance to all agencies on advisory committees. Furthermore, within FEMA already receiving substantial input from the fire service community at several levels. FEMA's Advisory Board includes representation from the fire service community. Moreover, USFA has a Board of Visitors composed of non-agency representatives of the fire service community. USFA also holds numerous meetings through the year with representatives from the major fire service organizations to receive their input. In addition, USFA leadership regularly attend and participate in major conferences conducted by the fire service community. Finally, USFA has opposed the proliferation of advisory boards and councils because of the expense associated with managing and organizing these boards and because of the often marginal value of the substantive work performed by these boards. We believe that the establishment of the United States Fire Advisory Council would duplicate existing efforts and require increased funding to support such a council; accordingly we are opposed to Section 3 and recommend its deletion.

Thank you, Mr. Chairman, for the opportunity to appear before the Subcommittee. I would be pleased to answer any questions you and the other members of the Subcommittee might have.

Mr. BOUCHER. Well, thank you very much, Administrator Brown, for that thorough and informative presentation. And, again, we welcome you back to this subcommittee.

I suppose the most recent new responsibility that we have provided to you is implementation of the Arson Prevention Act recently signed into law by the President. The appropriations conference report, as you probably know, has provided $2.5 million to implement that program for fiscal year 1995. Hopefully, we can anticipate at least that level of funding or perhaps slightly more for fiscal year 1996.

Just comment, if you will, about your plans for implementing that Act, any problems that you may foresee in doing so, and the adequacy of that level of funding and whether you think with that level of funding you can carry forward an adequate program in arson prevention.

Mrs. CARRYE BROWN. I want to let you know that we have drafted the regs and they are being published in the Federal Register. It is my understanding that they should be printed today and they are out for a 45-day comment period. I do believe that the amount of money that is, as I understand, in the appropriations is—we will be able to manage it and to the best of our abilities carry out what you all have mandated in the past for us to do.

Mr. BOUCHER. Okay. Well, that's excellent. I wasn't aware that you had gotten that far along with the regulation process and I am very pleased to hear that.

Mrs. CARRYE BROWN. Yes. Thank you.

Mr. BOUCHER. Let me just briefly comment on the question of the Advisory Council. I understand that the Administration has some reluctance to see new advisory commissions established with this degree of formality in the statute. And I'm also aware that the National Performance Review published by the Administration generally discourages councils, but they should not be seen as being discouraged in every instance.

What I understand the NPR to discourage is the establishment of advisory bodies that are permanent in nature, that do not have a limited life, that have the potential to simply drag on without offering important service but imposing costs with regard to the agency that has to carry them.

That certainly is not our intent with regard to the council we are recommending. It would have a very limited life of two years and is sunsetted after that point in time. It is very strongly supported by the fire services community that believes that, given advances in technology over the last 20 years, the current fiscal problems that your agency will face along with most others and the changing nature of the emergency response involving now much more in the field of hazardous materials than was the case in the past, that giving you this advice for a very limited period of two years helping you perhaps fine tune and redefine the mission of agency would be appropriate.

And I was particularly pleased to hear Mr. Weldon's enthusiastic endorsement of this council, and it does bear the unanimous support of the fire services community. So I understand where your statement comes from. We accept it in the spirit in which it's intended and we will go ahead and authorize the council anyway.

Now, Mrs. Brown, we appreciate you being with us and I would like now to recognize the gentleman from New York, Mr. Boehlert.

Mr. BOEHLERT. Thank you very much, Mr. Chairman. Welcome home, I think. Let me go a little bit afield and ask you a couple of things just for reaction.

Mrs. CARRYE BROWN. Sure.

Mr. BOEHLERT. One of the things that concerns me in talking with my volunteer companies back home is the difficulty in recruiting. Is this a problem that you are able to quantify as you look around the country? Is there anyone within your operation looking at this?

Mrs. CARRYE BROWN. I can probably say we are looking at that and we have been looking at it, from my understanding, for at least a year. We are going around the country looking at it. We do have a report out that deals with retention and recruitment. It is a tremendous problem within the volunteer service.

Mr. BOEHLERT. I would appreciate if you have the appropriate staff member give me some information on that because—

Mrs. CARRYE BROWN. I would be happy to do that.

Mr. BOEHLERT. The other thing that bothered me I read yesterday and I clipped it out. I read the paper—you remember the old days, I read the paper, clip them out and put them in my pocket to get to them in more detail later.

It seems to me in the last couple of days I read something about 12 of the fire fighters who volunteered to go out west to help fight the great forest fires who lost their lives and are not getting benefits because they are temporary employees. Good God, we should all wear black arm bands. What's the story there. I know it's not directly under your purview.

Mrs. CARRYE BROWN. As a matter of fact, it is a totally different agency. I don't really know a lot about it. They do employ hotshot individuals who go out and are dedicated for that but they are temporary employees. I think the analogy was made to the person that had a heart attack cleaning one of the monuments and didn't have any sort of insurance because they are temporary employees.

Mr. BOEHLERT. This fellow worked for eight years cleaning the Lincoln Memorial and he died on the job and got no benefits.

Mrs. CARRYE BROWN. Right.

Mr. BOEHLERT. That's a different agency. I understand that. But I hope you deplore it publicly from your lofty perch as I will, too, from this one.

Mrs. CARRYE BROWN. Thank you.

Mr. BOEHLERT. The final thing is the training at the Academy and the stipend program. I don't know the exact amount of the stipends these days, but are they adequate?

I remember during Reagan's days—which he was trying to cut everything, and I applauded many things that he proposed—I thought he was wacko. In this instance, he wanted to eliminate the stipends.

Are they adequate today, the stipends, for training at the Fire Academy? And is that an inducement maybe to help attract more recruits to the local companies with the thought that they are going to get paid training at the Academy?

Mrs. CARRYE BROWN. It is adequate, but there is such a demand to come to the Academy that it is very hard to fill the need. So what our organization is doing is trying to look at distance learning, to look at training the trainer and to try to see what other kinds of avenues and venues we can use to reach volunteer and career fire fighters out in the field. There is such a demand for coming in for the residential program.

Mr. BOEHLERT. Thank you, Mrs. Brown.

The recruitment thing is of great concern to me and obviously the training is of concern to all of us, so anything your staff might be able to share with me with on that, I would welcome. I just want to say by all of us previously, it's good to see you back here and we are so very pleased and proud to see you where you are today.

Mrs. CARRYE BROWN. Thank you very much.

Mr. BOEHLERT. Thank you very much.

Mr. BOUCHER. Thank you, Mr. Boehlert. The gentleman from California, Mr. Brown.

Mr. BROWN OF CALIFORNIA. Administrator Brown, I applaud your statement. I think it is excellent. I share, of course, the Chairman's views with regard to the Advisory Committee, but I understand the situation there. I particularly want to commend you on the emphasis you have placed on the research and technology aspects.

I don't want to go into it at this point, but I want to alert you to the fact that I will be following the developments there. I believe that the Fire Service, along with many other activities, can benefit a very great deal from enhanced research activities and the fact that you have a Chief Scientist to advise you in that area I think is very commendable and should bode well for the future of the fire program.

Just a demonstration or indication of the importance I attach to your testimony. I read every word of it and there's only one word that I found that I thought there was something wrong with it and I refer you to page 5, line 3, where I think you have a typo.

Would you confirm that, please?

Mrs. CARRYE BROWN. Page 5, line 3.

Mr. BROWN OF CALIFORNIA. You have the word confirmed there and I think you meant confined.

Mrs. CARRYE BROWN. I think you are right. Thank you, Mr. Chairman.

Mr. BROWN OF CALIFORNIA. That demonstrates I do read your testimony.

Thank you very much.

Mrs. CARRYE BROWN. Thank you very much.

Mr. BOUCHER. The gentlewoman from Texas, Mrs. Johnson.

Ms. JOHNSON OF TEXAS. Thank you, Mr. Chairman. I want to make a clarification with Representative Boehlert. I thought he mentioned the fire fighters—volunteer fire fighters because they were temporary employees. There are no benefits.

Mr. BOEHLERT. I was talking specifically with the fire fighters that were hired by the government to go out and help fight the fires out, the forest fires, and died on the job and are not getting benefits. That's absolutely crazy, working for the U.S. Government in a crisis situation.

Ms. JOHNSON OF TEXAS. I thought we always had employee mandates and employer mandates and portability with Federal Government benefits. We didn't have them there as well?

Thank you. Your opposition to the Advisory Council has to do with the costs and duplication of services you mentioned?

Mrs. CARRYE BROWN. Yes, ma'am.

Ms. JOHNSON OF TEXAS. Could you give me an idea of what you consider that cost to be, what portion or percentage of your total $31.4 million budget?

Mrs. CARRYE BROWN. I'm not exactly sure what percentage of the total budget, but I can tell you that the cost would be associated with actually bringing them to the Academy for meetings, that's some of the cost associated with that, and just all the staffing that goes with running an Advisory Council.

But if you would like to for the record, we can give you an estimate based on the Board of Visitors and their activities. We have a Board of Visitors for the National Fire Academy. We can base that and give you sort of an estimate.

I would be more than happy to provide that for the record.

Ms. JOHNSON OF TEXAS. And how would the responsibilities differ from the Board of Visitors and the Advisory Council.

Mrs. CARRYE BROWN. Well, see, that's a very good question. I think some of it would be overlapping and that would be something that we would have to explore. That's a very good question.

Ms. JOHNSON OF TEXAS. Could they be combined?

Mrs. CARRYE BROWN. That's a very interesting question. That's a very interesting suggestion.

Ms. JOHNSON OF TEXAS. Thank you.

Mr. BOUCHER. Thank you, Ms. Johnson.

Mr. Barca.

Mr. BARCA. Thank you for being here before our committee and I appreciate the work that your division is doing. One question that I thought I'd ask that actually came from the staff suggestion, but it seemed like a good one to me, was the idea of asking whether or not students that go through the program complete evaluations of that program and what you've learned from those evaluations. Have they—and how you've incorporated those into your training programs.

Mrs. CARRYE BROWN. We have, to my delight, a very strong evaluation process and it does include the students. I think they do an evaluation immediately afterwards, and three to six months down the line as well. And what we've found from them is that they enjoy coming.

And the interchange of ideas from other fire fighters from around the country, that's what's extremely valuable to them. Not only that we have an 800 number, we bring the fire organizations in for a two-day period to critique our programs, to tell us what they do or they don't like about it. Then we have experts from around the country as well giving us advice and guidance on our activities and programs. And we change the programs based on a multifaceted approach to evaluating and getting evaluations.

Mr. BARCA. Very good. I know that I've heard nothing but positive feedback from my district as I get around to the various fire departments, so there has been a high degree of praise here.

The other question I have deals with the idea of using modern information technologies today. What degree have you been able to—has that been able to enable you to speed up the delivery of new information that's coming out in terms of new research on fire saving techniques and things of that support?

Mrs. CARRYE BROWN. It is a goal of mine to further expanding that for using computers to download and get information out. We have simulation labs as well, and I would like to look at more distance learning activities and the use of satellites to get information out to remote areas so they will not have to come in and we can meet some of the demands of Fire Service communities around the country.

Mr. BARCA. Have you done that to any degree so far with, let's say, distance learning kinds of activities.

Mrs. CARRYE BROWN. Yes, we have. And I'll be happy to provide that for you for the record. We have done a great deal of it and there's more on-line that we have done. As a matter of fact, let's see, Jim Coyle is here and the—the reason why at this moment I can't remember some of the things that we have done. I would like to allow my deputy superintendent to tell you some of the distance learning activities that we have done because I don't want to shortchange that. That's very important.

Mr. BOUCHER. Mr. Coyle, could you state your name please for the record and your position at the agency.

Mr. COYLE. James Coyle, Deputy Superintendent of the National Fire Academy. Thank you. We have a number of programs that include both the use of the television medium through the EENET programs. That is a basically a FEMA program, but the Fire Administration and the Fire Academy have been heavy users of that and we are looking at new ways in which we will use the EENET broadcasting capabilities for life interaction with the Fire Service.

In addition, we are in the process now of developing a lot of new technology for the instant command training that's necessary between both the Fire Service at instant response, as well as the EOC operations. We are working very closely and are developing a couple of hand-off packages that will convert that instant command program on a CD-ROM program that we can hand off directly to the fire services currently in development. And we are getting a lot of specific input from the Fire Service on that.

Related to that is an issue of fire-safe building design which has been a real concern, not only for the Fire Service, but architects and engineers and others in the community. That is another program that is in development on CD-ROM and that will be a handoff package into the field. So we will be extending more and more of those technical capabilities that we develop through our courses.

Then in a lower technology way, we share practically all of our courses to the Fire Service, either through direct deliveries, Train the Trainer as Mrs. Brown has mentioned, or through our regional delivery programs. And all those materials are made available, including video and tapes and the other supporting documentation. Plus we make the list of the Academy instructors available so they can use our people who have been trained and tested by the National Fire Academy.

There's a whole range of other things in the development stage that we are looking at as well, so I think we are making a fairly significant shift that started a couple of years ago and moving more in the direction of distance learning that Mrs. Brown has talked about.

Mr. BARCA. Very good. I appreciate hearing that feedback. I haven't heard quite as much on that program from my various fire departments. I get around and visit with them, and I will have to bring some of this to their attention as well. So I appreciate the information.

Mrs. CARRYE BROWN. Thank you for the question.

Mr. BOUCHER. Mr. Coyle, let me just ask a brief follow-up to that if I may. It is an interesting inquiry. Among the other things this subcommittee does is helping to fashion a Federal role in research and development that helps advance the information infrastructure and interactive technology is of great interest to us.

You said that you are considering a wider employment of distance learning and I suppose electronic classrooms. Will those be interactive in nature where you utilize a satellite or microwave technology to have a course taught at a central location then received by a variety of firemen around the country?

Mr. COYLE. We just had, in fact, two weeks ago someone in the private sector who is doing that now, who's approached the Academy for trying to put our courses on-line in interactive cable networks. So that's the future, as you know, and much of this in the educational context, so we are looking at all that.

Obviously, since we are looking for a long-term development for the Academy, we want to be very careful in what approaches we use, given our limited resources and the ability to make sure we are equitable in making those courses available to both volunteer and the paid Fire Service across the country because we will run into some of those same problems of access in the volunteer service that we have now with our programs. So we are very concerned about that.

The exciting thing, as far as the current development in the instant command area is, we actually have a three-phase plan. The fourth phase—the third phase on that is literally to go on-line with the State and local Fire Service interests and be able to do interactive, incident-based scenario training from the Academy, tying in the local Fire Service as well as our FEMA partners at the national level. That's already in the planning stage.

Mr. BOUCHER. Are you getting advice from, for example, rural volunteer fire services as to what kinds of electronically transmitted training would meet their needs the best, whether that be CD-ROM which is really not interactive, it is just a matter of an efficient means to show them the material that you have or whether something that is truly interactive would be better? Were you hearing from them?

Mr. COYLE. We've had some of that, not as much as we want to do. I think Mrs. Brown has already alluded to our focus groups. We are actually going to go out into the field this year and do focus groups of the volunteer Fire Service. In the past, most of our focus groups have been—while they are on campus, what we want to do is go out into the field and get with the allied professions that interface with the volunteer fire services in the community and find out what assets are available so we can take advantage of all of those. That's in our planning. We are hoping to get into that this coming fiscal year.

Mr. BOUCHER. And maybe this is a way that the new council can assist you in your activities.

Mr. COYLE. That's Mrs. Brown's activities.

Mr. BOUCHER. Thank you, Mr. Coyle. And Mrs. Brown, thank you very much for your presence here this morning.

Mr. Barca.

Mr. BARCA. I'm sorry. I apologize. I came a little bit late. There was just one other question I thought maybe I'd ask and that was in your testimony, as I was reviewing it, I had read how you had indicated that we had made progress in bringing down the number of deaths from fire over the past few decades which is something we should all be proud of. Then you also alluded to the fact that comparatively to other industrialized nations, that our statistics are relatively high.

I'm wondering, have you done some work in this area—is there some more—have we really spent some time to looking at efforts of other nations? Is it due to construction techniques they use? Is it due to programs, the practices of people individually in terms of their efforts in fire safety?

Where are there areas that we should be looking towards as a Nation and as individual States and communities to really make a dent to learn from the experiences from other nations, I guess?

Mrs. CARRYE BROWN. The USFA has sponsored studies on that for a number of years. But what you find is that our attitude about fire—we have a different attitude about fire than all of the other nations around the country. And I think studies were done in Europe and Japan and I think, largely, its educating the public about fire, letting them know about things they ought to be watching out for, explaining to them what they should do in a fire situation.

So those—that's the primary reason why we have a different sort of a problem simply because of our attitude about fire. It's a different attitude. They are aware over there in Europe and Japan and they understand what fires can do. We have not had one actually here, just by ones and twos people are dying, and we just don't have the same sort of appreciation for what it can do.

Mr. BARCA. Thank you.

Mr. BOUCHER. Thank you, Mr. Barca.

And Mrs. Brown, again, thank you for being with us today, and we look forward to working with you as we together fashion a more appropriate Federal response to the problems that we face in terms of deaths and loss of property by fire.

Mrs. CARRYE BROWN. Thank you. I look forward to working with you.

Mr. BOUCHER. That concludes the hearing phase of our proceedings this morning. The subcommittee is adjourned for purposes of the hearing and reconvened for purposes of marking up the legislation which is before us.

[Whereupon, at 10:42 a.m., the subcommittee was proceeded to other business.]

SUBCOMMITTEE MARKUP—THE FEDERAL FIRE PREVENTION AND CONTROL ACT AUTHORIZATION

TUESDAY, SEPTEMBER 20, 1994

HOUSE OF REPRESENTATIVES,
COMMITTEE ON SCIENCE, SPACE, AND TECHNOLOGY,
SUBCOMMITTEE ON SCIENCE,
Washington, D.C.

The subcommittee met, pursuant to call, at 10:42 a.m. in Room 2318, Rayburn House Office Building, Hon. Rick Boucher [chairman of the subcommittee] presiding.

Mr. BOUCHER. The Chair now calls up before the subcommittee the subcommittee print for markup. The print is before the Members and a section-by-section analysis of the proposed bill is also before the Members.

[The information follows:]

F:\M\BOUCHE\BOUCHE.088 H.L.C.

[SUBCOMMITTEE PRINT]

SEPTEMBER 12, 1994

103D CONGRESS
2D SESSION

H. R. ______

IN THE HOUSE OF REPRESENTATIVES

Mr. BOUCHER introduced the following bill; which was referred to the Committee on ______________________

A BILL

To authorize appropriations for activities under the Federal Fire Prevention and Control Act of 1974, and for other purposes.

Be it enacted by the Senate and House of Representatives of the United States of America in Congress assembled,

SECTION 1. SHORT TITLE.

This Act may be cited as the "Fire Administration Authorization Act of 1994".

SEC. 2. AUTHORIZATION OF APPROPRIATIONS.

Section 17(g)(1) of the Federal Fire Prevention and Control Act of 1974 (15 U.S.C. 2215(g)(1)) is amended—

(1) by striking "and" at the end of subparagraph (E);

(2) by striking the period at the end of subparagraph (F) and inserting in lieu thereof a semicolon; and

(3) by adding at the end the following new subparagraphs:

"(G) $31,490,000 for the fiscal year ending September 30, 1995;

"(H) $31,490,000 for the fiscal year ending September 30, 1996; and

"(I) $31,490,000 for the fiscal year ending September 30, 1997.".

SEC. 3. UNITED STATES FIRE ADVISORY COUNCIL.

(a) ESTABLISHMENT.—(1) The Administrator of the United States Fire Administration (in this section referred to as "Administrator") shall establish the United States Fire Advisory Council (in this section referred to as the "Council").

(2) The Council shall consist of not more than 12 members, to be appointed by the Administrator to reflect a broad cross-section of the fire and emergency services community, including members of both the paid and vol-

unteer fire services, and including 1 member selected from among the members of the Board of Visitors of the National Fire Academy.

(3) The Administrator shall appoint from among the members of the Council a chairperson and vice-chairperson. The Council shall meet not less than 2 times in any calendar year.

(b) FUNCTIONS.—The Council shall advise the Administrator on all matters related to the United States Fire Administration, and on—

(1) steps that should be taken to achieve the goals and priorities set forth in the report issued by the National Commission on Fire Prevention and Control on May 4, 1973, entitled "America Burning"; and

(2) any revisions in such goals and priorities which should be made because of advances in technology, the resource constraints of State and local governments, the changing nature of the emergency response services, or other factors considered appropriate by the Council.

(c) ADMINISTRATION.—Members of the Council shall serve without compensation but shall be allowed travel expenses, including per diem in lieu of subsistence, as authorized by law, including subchapter I of chapter 57 of title 5, United States Code, and section 7(d) of the Federal Advisory Committee Act, for persons serving intermittently in government service.

(d) SUNSET.—The Council shall cease to exist 2 years after the date of enactment of this Act.

SECTIONAL ANALYSIS OF SUBCOMMITTEE PRINT REAUTHORIZATION OF FEDERAL FIRE PREVENTION AND CONTROL ACT OF 1974

Section 1. Short Title

The Act may be cited as the "Fire Administration Authorization Act of 1994."

Section 2. Authorization of Appropriations

Authorizes $31,490,000 in each of fiscal years 1995, 1996, and 1997, for the programs and activities of the Federal Fire Prevention and Control Act of 1974. These programs and activities include public education on fire prevention and control; the collection and analysis of data relating to fire; research and development in fire suppression; the promotion of firefighter health and safety; and the administration of the National Fire Academy in Emmitsburg, Maryland.

Section 3. United States Fire Advisory Council

Establishes a twelve-person advisory council to advise the U.S. Fire Administrator on: 1) how well the nation is achieving the broad goals set forth in 1974 by the National Commission on Fire Prevention and Control, and 2) whether the Commissions goals and priorities should be adjusted because of the changing nature of the emergency response services.

U.S. FIRE ADMINISTRATION HISTORICAL FUNDING
(dollars in millions)

FY	BUDGET AUTH.	REQUESTS	ACTUAL OBLIGATIONS
89	$17.03	$15.043	$18.855
90	$17.73	$15.667	$19.669
91	$18.46	$20.394	$24.404
92	$25.55	$28.651	$30.634
93	$26.62	$26.344	$33.807
94	$27.52	$37.181	$31.490*
95	$31.49**	$31.490	--
96	$31.49**	--	--
97	$31.49**	--	--

Changes from request:

1990 Reflects Congressional increases for printing First Responder course materials, stipends and Fire Prevention and Arson Control.
1991 Reflects Congressional increases for National Emergency Training Center (NETC) renovation and Training Field Deployment Programs.
1992 Reflects Congressional increases for NETC renovation and Hazardous Materials Training Center in Vermont and Iowa.
1993 Reflects Congressional increases for NETC renovation, Title III and the Vermont Hazardous Materials training center. An additional agency increase due to the transfer of the Hazardous Materials Division to USFA.
1994 Reflects a decrease due to the reorganization of FEMA, which transferred the Hazardous Materials Division including Title III activities and The Emergency Education Network (EENET) program to the Preparedness, Training and Exercises Directorate.

*Reflects current year allocation to USFA
**Requested authorization level

Mr. BOUCHER. As I indicated in the opening statement, the proposed legislation has two parts. First, it authorizes for the next three years the programs and activities of the Federal Fire Prevention and Control Act of 1974 at a level of $31.49 million for each of those years. This is a hard freeze at fiscal year 1994 levels.

Secondly, after close consultations with the fire services community, the proposed legislation establishes a U.S. Fire Advisory Council for a two-year period to assess how effectively the Nation is meeting the goals and priorities of the original "America Burning" report and to determine whether changes should be made in those goals and priorities given advances that have been made and new needs that have arisen in the intervening time.

The description I think was adequate in my opening statement at the hearing. Therefore, at this time, I will simply insert in the record a more lengthy description and recognize the gentleman from New York, Mr. Boehlert, whose steadfast leadership in this arena we very much appreciate.

[The information follows:]

STATEMENT FOR MARK-UP
CHAIRMAN RICK BOUCHER (D-VA)
BEFORE THE SCIENCE SUBCOMMITTEE
ON THE REAUTHORIZATION OF THE FEDERAL FIRE
PREVENTION AND CONTROL ACT OF 1974
SEPTEMBER 20, 1994

The Chair now calls up the Subcommittee Print for mark-up. The Subcommittee Print is before the members as is a section-by-section analysis of the proposed bill.

As I indicated in my opening statement for the hearing, the proposed legislation has two parts:

First, it authorizes for the next three years the programs and activities of the Federal Fire Prevention and Control Act of 1974 at a level of $31.49 million in each of those years. This is ~~essentially a~~ a hard freeze at fiscal year 1994 levels.

Second, after close consultations with the fire services community, the proposed legislation would establish a U.S. Fire Advisory Council to asses how effectively the nation is meeting the goals and priorities of the orginal ***America Burning*** report and to determine whether changes should be made in those goals and priorities.

I think my opening statement and the ensuing testimony and discussion about this bill adequately described the bill, so I will at this time recognize the gentlemen from New York, Mr. Boehlert, whose steadfast leadership in the area of fire safety has certainly made this a safer nation for millions of Americans.

Mr. BOEHLERT. Mr. Chairman, I think we are ready to move. Your statement quite adequately explained the provisions of the bill and we certainly know of its necessity and we've just had a very good hearing to express the importance, so I think we are ready to go and the bill should be opened at this point for amendment.

Mr. BOUCHER. All right. Without objection, the bill will be considered as original text for the purposes of markup and, without objection, it will be open for amendment at any point. And the Chair asks if any Member has an amendment to the bill.

Hearing none, the Chair is pleased to recognize the gentleman from New York, Mr. Boehlert, for a motion.

Mr. BOEHLERT. Mr. Chairman, I move that the subcommittee report the bill. Furthermore, I move to instruct the staff to prepare the subcommittee report, to make any necessary technical and conforming amendments, and that the Chairman take all necessary steps to bring the bill before the full committee for consideration.

Mr. BOUCHER. The question is on the motion of the gentleman from New York.

Those in favor will say aye.

Those opposed, no.

The ayes have it and the motion is agreed to and the bill is reported in accordance with the terms of the motion.

And I want to congratulate the subcommittee on what I think is a record time for reporting legislation. And with that, this subcommittee markup session is adjourned.

[Whereupon, at 10:45 a.m., the subcommittee was adjourned.]

APPENDIX

HOYER TESTIMONY BEFORE THE SCIENCE SUBCOMMITTEE
HOUSE SCIENCE, SPACE AND TECHNOLOGY COMMITTEE
HR 2318, THE FEDERAL FIRE PREVENTION AND CONTROL ACT

AS THE CHAIRMAN OF THE CONGRESSIONAL FIRE SERVICES CAUCUS, I WANT TO THANK CHAIRMAN BOUCHER AND CONGRESSMAN BOEHLERT FOR THEIR CONTINUED EFFORTS ON BEHALF OF OUR COUNTRY'S FIRE AND EMERGENCY PERSONNEL. FEW MEMBERS WORK HARDER ON THESE ISSUES THAN BOTH OF YOU, AND I KNOW THAT THE FIRE CAUCUS AND THE MEN AND WOMEN WHO WORK EACH DAY TO MAKE OUR COMMUNITIES SAFE GREATLY VALUE YOUR CONTINUED COMMITMENT.

HAVING SAID THAT, I BRING GREETINGS FROM THE 370 MEMBERS OF THE FIRE CAUCUS, AND HOPE TO ADD MY THOUGHTS TO THE FIRE ADMINISTRATION AUTHORIZATION BEFORE YOUR COMMITTEE TODAY.

ALTHOUGH FIRE AND EMERGENCY RESPONSE IS LARGELY A LOCAL ISSUE, THE FEDERAL GOVERNMENT HAS AN IMPORTANT ROLE TO PLAY HERE. THAT ROLE IS DEFINED AND MOLDED BY THE LEGISLATION BEFORE US TODAY. IF WE WANT TO CONTINUE TO PROVIDE FEDERAL LEADERSHIP ON FIRE AND EMERGENCY ISSUES, WE WILL STRONGLY SUPPORT LEGISLATION WHICH SUPPORTS THE FIRE ADMINISTRATION.

CLEARLY, THERE IS A NEED FOR FEDERAL LEADERSHIP ON THESE ISSUES. DESPITE GREAT STRIDES DURING THE LAST TWO DECADES IN HALVING THE PER CAPITA DEATH RATE, WE STILL LOSE TOO MANY AMERICANS TO THE RAVAGES OF FIRE. JUST UNDER 6,000 AMERICANS ARE KILLED EACH YEAR BY FIRE, AND MOST OF THESE DEATHS TAKE PLACE AMONGST OUR COUNTRY'S MOST VULNERABLE POPULATIONS: CHILDREN AND THE ELDERLY. IN ADDITION, NEARLY 29,000 PEOPLE ARE INJURED EACH YEAR BY FIRE. COMPARED TO THE HUMAN ELEMENT OF OUR COUNTRY'S FIRE PROBLEM, THE BILLIONS OF DOLLARS IN LOST PROPERTY AND BUSINESS SEEMS LESS IMPORTANT, THOUGH IT CERTAINLY IMPACTS THE QUALITY OF LIFE FOR MANY PEOPLE IN COMMUNITIES ACROSS OUR COUNTRY.

FOR ALL OF THESE REASONS, I OFFER MY STRONG SUPPORT FOR THE LEGISLATION BEFORE US TODAY, AND WOULD LIKE TO ADDRESS MY REMARKS TO BOTH THE FUNDING LEVEL CALLED FOR IN THE LEGISLATION, AND THE PROPOSED FIRE ADVISORY COUNCIL.

FIRST, I WOULD LIKE TO SAY THAT AS THE CHAIRMAN OF THE FIRE CAUCUS, I WOULD LIKE TO SEE MORE FUNDING FOR THE FIRE ADMINISTRATION. I BELIEVE THE TRAINING PROGRAMS OFFERED BY THE NATIONAL FIRE ACADEMY, UNDER THE FIRE ADMINISTRATION, TRANSLATE INTO BETTER PROTECTION FOR LOCAL COMMUNITIES. MOREOVER, I BELIEVE THE FIRE PREVENTION EFFORTS AND DATA COLLECTION CONDUCTED BY THE FIRE ADMINISTRATION TRANSLATE INTO A BETTER EDUCATED CITIZENRY WHO WILL BE BETTER PREPARED FOR FIRE AND OTHER EMERGENCIES WHEN THEY OCCUR.

IN FACT, JUST THIS YEAR, WE PASSED THE ARSON PREVENTION ACT, THANKS TO THE HARD WORK OF CHAIRMAN BOUCHER AND CONGRESSMAN BOEHLERT, WHICH COULD NOT BE FULLY FUNDED BECAUSE OF FUNDING CONSTRAINTS. I WOULD LIKE TO SEE FUTURE FIRE ADMINISTRATION BUDGETS TAKE INTO ACCOUNT THE MONEY AUTHORIZED BY THIS BILL. NEVERTHELESS, I RECOGNIZE THE DIFFICULT POSITION IN WHICH FEMA, THE FIRE ADMINISTRATION, AND THIS COMMITTEE FIND THEMSELVES. THERE IS TOO LITTLE MONEY FOR TOO MANY GOOD PROGRAMS.

CONSEQUENTLY, I BELIEVE THE COMMITTEE HAS DRAFTED A REASONABLE FUNDING REQUEST IN LIGHT OF THE BUDGETARY CONSTRAINTS WE ARE ALL FACING, AND THAT THIS BUDGET WILL CONTINUE TO PROVIDE THE LEVEL OF SUPPORT WE NEED TO ENSURE THAT THE FEDERAL GOVERNMENT REMAINS A PLAYER IN FIRE ISSUES. HOWEVER, I DO NOT BELIEVE WE CAN AFFORD TO REDUCE THE FUNDING FOR THE FIRE ADMINISTRATION BELOW THE HARD FREEZE CALLED FOR IN THIS BILL WITHOUT SERIOUSLY IMPACTING PROGRAM INTEGRITY.

SECONDLY, I THINK THE CREATION OF A FIRE ADVISORY COUNCIL TO ADVISE THE FIRE ADMINISTRATOR AND THE NATION ON HOW WELL WE ARE MEETING THE CHALLENGES SET FORTH BY THE NATIONAL COMMISSION ON FIRE PREVENTION AND CONTROL MAKES SENSE. WE MUST CONTINUE TO HOLD OUR FEET TO THE FIRE, SO TO SPEAK. WE NEED TO WORK TOWARD CONCRETE AND EASILY IDENTIFIABLE GOALS, AND WE NEED TO HAVE SOME OBJECTIVE MARKER OF WHERE WE STAND IN ACHIEVING THOSE GOALS. A NATIONAL ADVISORY COUNCIL WILL PROVIDE THAT.

IN CONCLUSION, I THINK THE FIRE ADMINISTRATION AUTHORIZATION BILL BEFORE US TODAY IS A GOOD BILL FOR THE FIRE ADMINISTRATION, THE FIRE AND EMERGENCY PERSONNEL OF OUR COUNTRY, AND THE AMERICAN PUBLIC. I WANT TO CONGRATULATE THE COMMITTEE ON ITS WORK, AND I LOOK FORWARD TO WORKING WITH YOU FURTHER TO PROMOTE OUR FEDERAL COMMITMENT TO THE FIRE AND EMERGENCY SERVICES.

INTERNATIONAL ASSOCIATION OF ARSON INVESTIGATORS, INC.

300 South Broadway, Suite 100 St. Louis, MO 63102 Phone 314/621-1966 Fax 314/621-5125

Please reply to:
P. O. Box 5070
Wilmington, DE 199808

September 19, 1994

Honorable Rick Boucher
Chairman Subcommittee on Science
United States House of Representatives
Suite 2320 Rayburn House Office Building
Washington, DC 20515-6301

ATTN: Mr. Paul Regan

Dear Congressman Boucher:

This letter is in response to your letter of August 25, 1994 directed to John Barracato, President of the International Association of Arson Investigators.

Mr. Barracato has authorized me to respond.

It is the position of the International Association of Arson Investigators to support the Fire Authorization Act.

Should this Act become law, we trust that the United States Fire Advisory Council include at least one representative that represents the interest of fire and arson investigators.

Thank you for allowing us to comment on this important legislation.

Please do not hesitate to contact me if I can provide any further information.

Sincerely,

Stephen P. Austin

Stephen P. Austin
External Affairs Representative

cc: IAAI Executive Officers

SPA/pp 01/0919003

INTERNATIONAL ASSOCIATION of ARSON INVESTIGATORS INC.
IAAI

NFPA®

National Fire Protection Association
International

Executive Offices
1 Batterymarch Park
P.O. Box 9101
Quincy, Massachusetts 02269-9101 USA
Telephone (617) 770-3000 Fax (617) 770-0700

Washington Office
Suite 560, 1110 N. Glebe Road
Arlington, VA 22201
Telephone: (703) 516-4346
Fax: (703) 516-4350

Statement of the

National Fire Protection Association

to the

Honorable Rick Boucher, Chairman
Subcommittee on Science/Committee on
Science, Space and Technology
U.S. House of Representatives

Fire Administration Authorization Act of 1994

September 20, 1994

Presented by:
Anthony R. O'Neill
Vice President
Government Affairs

The National Fire Protection Association (NFPA) appreciates the opportunity to submit this statement in support of the "Fire Administration Authorization Act of 1994" and to discuss other relevant issues concerning the United States Fire Administration and the National Fire Academy (NFA).

We commend you, Mr. Chairman, both for holding this important hearing today and for your dedicated leadership in fire safety issues. It has been a privilege working with you over the years and we look forward to continuing our joint efforts towards a safer America.

Overview of NFPA

The NFPA which will celebrate its 100th anniversary in 1996 has as its mission the safeguarding of people, their property, and the environment from destructive fire and related hazards, through scientific and engineering techniques and education. With over 60,000 members representing the fire service, health care, business and industry, insurance, architects, fire equipment manufacturers and Federal, state and local governments, NFPA represents a wide variety of interests but all with the same goal and concerns, that of improving fire safety throughout the United States. Because of the nature of our work and our mission, the NFPA has a vital interest in the future success of the United States Fire Administration (USFA), and the programs of the National Fire Academy (NFA).

USFA/NFA Funding

NFPA was a member of the National Commission on Fire Prevention and Control that recommended the creation of the USFA. Acting on the findings of the Commission,

Congress passed the Federal Fire Prevention and Control Act in 1974. Through the past two decades, funding for the USFA has been up and down. We have come before Congress numerous times in support of additional funding for the fire and emergency training programs conducted by the USFA and the NFA and we do so again today. We are disappointed that the Administration's requests are level funded for the next three years.

Fire statistics still show the US with one of the highest fire death rates per capita among industrialized nations. It is an embarrassment. This year's request of $31,490,000 is not enough to do all that needs to be done. Recent increases in funding have allowed the fire administration to strengthen its programs but more is still needed.

In the past, shortage of funds has prevented the USFA from undertaking special studies which would provide valuable research to the fire service community. In order to make advances in technology and meet the constantly changing needs of the fire and emergency medical services - we depend on you, Mr. Chairman and members of the Subcommittee, to request an increase in funding for fiscal years 1995, 1996 and 1997.

The NFPA strongly supports and urges the Subcommittee to increase funding for USFA and NFA programs.

FEMA/USFA Leadership
Director James Lee Witt and Administrator Carrye Brown are to be commended for their commitment to the goals they have set out to achieve. NFPA supports their efforts. By providing a Federal focus on the Nation's fire problem,

the USFA has supported and provided many benefits to the fire protection community. And in return, the fire service has throughout the years forged an alliance to help assure the United States Fire Administration and the National Fire Academy continue to play a prominent role. We believe this authorization bill provides yet another opportunity for the fire protection community to help guide the future success of the Fire Administration.

"United States Fire Advisory Council"
The establishment of the "United States Fire Advisory Council" to counsel the Administrator and assess the goals established by America Burning is a concept with merit that deserves careful consideration. NFPA favors having a member of the Board of Visitors of the National Fire Academy as a member of the "fire council". The fire service wants to be assured that the Fire Academy will continue to put out the best courses and curriculum material to instruct and train fire service and emergency personnel.

Public Education
NFPA has enjoyed a long term cooperative relationship with the USFA. We have relied on each other to supplement and heighten our mutual efforts in community outreach programs. We look forward to working with the USFA to assure that effective programs are not diminished. NFPA prides itself in its educational programs including the Learn Not to Burn® fire safety education materials which are widely implemented in preschool and elementary schools throughout the United States and Canada. With limited resources in both the public and private sectors, any fire safety campaign undertaken by the Federal government must not duplicate or conflict with existing private sector

programs. We therefore look forward to collaborating with the USFA to fulfill unmet needs. The more we can work together to deliver clear, consistent fire safety messages to the public, the better.

We would like to bring to the Subcommittee's attention an excellent example of a partnership success namely the one between the NFPA, USFA, and the Los Angeles Fire Department in the creation of the School Outreach Program. The result of the shocking L.A. Riots in May 1992, the program teaches inner-city children in Los Angeles about fire safety using the Learn Not to Burn® educational materials as a base. Curriculum materials were translated into Spanish to meet the needs of the community. It also teaches children self-esteem by emphasizing good citizenship and strong character.

In cases where the information already exists the public would be well served if the Federal government put its resources where they are most needed - in getting existing materials and information distributed.

National Fire Incident Reporting System (NFIRS)
The USFA's operation of the National Fire Incident Reporting System (NFIRS) provides an essential element in the nation's ability to track our progress in reducing the toll from unwanted fire. Accurate, detailed analysis of the key patterns in our fire experience would not be possible without NFIRS.

With literally thousands of cooperating state and local fire agencies and tens of thousands of individuals contributing reports to the data base, NFIRS is also the USFA's largest and most successful example of Federal/state/local government cooperation. And because the most valid use

' NFIRS also requires use of data from NFPA's annual ırvey, NFIRS-based analysis is also a good example of the nportance and success of public/private cooperation. But FIRS has also been a victim of the under-funding of the SFA in the past decade. Budgets have been sufficient to eep the system running but not to support training, /stem enhancements and data analysis to keep the system ılly viable in today's age of information technology. ecisions are only as good as the information available to ıpport them, and so our country needs a strong NFIRS -- ; strong as it once was and can be again.

FPA prides itself on its own fire experience data collection ıd analysis efforts. We have been pleased to provide the ongress and others with focused statistics to inform ecision-making on a wide range of critical fire safety issues. ut we could not have done so without the data produced y the USFA's NFIRS system.

IFPA has been pleased to cooperate with the USFA on many spects of fire data collection and analysis, just as we have n all the other programs I have described. We hope to do ven more together, thanks to the leadership of Carrye rown and her team.

:onclusion

Ve support the Subcommittee's work and would be happy ɔ provide any assistance necessary to ensure that fire afety and fire prevention receive the appropriate national ttention.

09/19/94 15:49 ☎302 995 6330 STATE FARM

INTERNATIONAL ASSOCIATION OF ARSON INVESTIGATORS, INC

300 South Broadway, Suite 100 St. Louis, MO 63102 Phone 314/621-1966 Fax 314/621-5

Please reply to:
P. O. Box 5070
Wilmington, DE 199808

September 19, 1994

Honorable Rick Boucher
Chairman Subcommittee on Science
United States House of Representatives
Suite 2320 Rayburn House Office Building
Washington, DC 20515-6301

ATTN: Mr. Paul Regan

Dear Congressman Boucher:

This letter is in response to your letter of August 25, 1994 directed to John Barracato, President of the International Association of Arson Investigators.

Mr. Barracato has authorized me to respond.

It is the position of the International Association of Arson Investigators to support the Fire Authorization Act.

Should this Act become law, we trust that the United States Fire Advisory Council include at least one representative that represents the interest of fire and arson investigators.

Thank you for allowing us to comment on this important legislation.

Please do not hesitate to contact me if I can provide any further information.

Sincerely,

Stephen P Austin/hm

Stephen P. Austin
External Affairs Representative

cc: IAAI Executive Officers

SPA/pp 01/0919003

INTERNATIONAL ASSOCIATION OF FIRE FIGHTERS

ALFRED K. WHITEHEAD
General President

VINCENT J. BOLLON
General Secretary-Treasurer

STATEMENT

ON

LEGISLATION REAUTHORIZING THE U.S. FIRE ADMINISTRATION

BEFORE THE

SUBCOMMITTEE ON SCIENCE

OF THE

HOUSE COMMITTEE ON SCIENCE, SPACE AND TECHNOLOGY

SEPTEMBER 20, 1994

BY

ALFRED K. WHITEHEAD

GENERAL PRESIDENT

50 NEW YORK AVENUE, N.W., WASHINGTON, D.C. 20006-5395 • (202) 737-8484 • FAX (202) 737-8418

Mr. Chairman, my name is Alfred K. Whitehead, and I am the General President of the International Association of Fire Fighters. I appear before you today on behalf of the more than 200,000 professional fire fighters and emergency medical personnel who comprise our International to express o strong support for your proposal reauthorizing the United States Fire Administration.

We wish to specifically offer our endorsement for the creation of an advisor council to consult with the Fire Administrator on all matters relating to the mission of the Administration. Not since the landmark **America Burning** was published in 1974 has there been an effort to bring together the diverge fire community to take a serious look at fire-related issues. While we do nc believe that a full fledged commission similar to the one that produced **America Burning** is needed at this time, we feel that now is an appropriate time to revisit the findings of the National Commission on Fire Preventio and Control to assess what progress has been made in the past twenty years.

In many ways, America in the 1990s is a far different place than America in the 1970s. Technological advances and a greater understanding of such dangers as hazardous materials and infectious diseases over the past 20 year will enable us to more effectively address some of the problems identified b the 1974 Commission. In addition, the delivery of emergency medical services needs to be carefully examined. The role of the fire service in EMS both growing and changing quite rapidly, and the proposed advisory counci would be in an ideal position to help the Fire Administration fully explore these developments.

As I am sure you are aware, Mr. Chairman, the diversity of the fire community will make the work of your proposed council difficult. When very divergent interests come together, consensus is often elusive. But this diversity is precisely the reason why the advisory council concept may be needed at this time. Under the auspices of the federal government, I believe that these organizations, which often find themselves at odds on a variety of issues, will be able to put aside their parochial concerns in an effort to take an honest look at the status of fire protection in our nation today.

Finally, I feel obliged to stress that our support of this advisory council should in no way be construed as any lack of faith in the incumbent Administrator. On the contrary, we feel that U.S. Fire Administrator Carrye Brown is doing a superb job, and we are excited about her efforts to reinvigorate an agency that has sometimes seemed to have forgotten its true mission.

It is precisely because Administrator Brown is on board that we are so eager to join with our brethren in the fire service community to reassess where we have been and where we are going. Carrye Brown has a proven track record of bringing the fire service groups together, and we believe that she will play a crucial role in enabling the work of the council to be productive and valuable.

As always, Mr. Chairman, your attention to the views of the International Association of Fire Fighters is greatly appreciated. I would be happy to answer any questions you may have.

Comments For The Record On

DISCUSSION DRAFT OF FIRE AUTHORIZATION ACT

At the hearing of the Science Subcommittee of the House Science, Space & Technology Committee
Rep. Rick Boucher, Chair

September 20, 1994

We are pleased to submit the following comments on the draft legislation to reauthorize the U. S. Fire Administration on behalf of the members of the Alliance for Fire and Emergency Management. The Alliance is an organization consisting of six professional associations: Fire and Injury Prevention Association, Professional Emergency Educators Association, Industrial Fire & Emergency Management Training Association, Hazardous Materials Responders & Educators Association, Fire Officers Association, and the Fire Department Safety Officers Association. The Alliance represents members engaged in activities across a broad cross section of fire, pre-hospital emergency care and emergency management services. We appreciate the opportunity to address important issues to America's emergency services.

In February 1993, the International Society of Fire Service Instructors (ISFSI), the creator of The Alliance, released its paper "Implementing America Burning: The Final Attempt" to the Clinton Administration, the leadership of the Federal Fire Program and to the fire service community. Contained in the paper are a series of far-reaching recommendations for establishing an effective Fire Prevention and Control Program at the federal level as identified by the National Commission on Fire Prevention and Control in its 1973 report, "America Burning."

ISFSI committed over three months to the preparation of the paper "Implementing America Burning," soliciting input from members of the fire service community throughout the country. We believe that the recommendations in our paper are as valid today as they were eighteen months ago when the report was released.

The ISFSI report contains over 100 recommendations. Several relate directly to the USFA and the National Fire Academy which should be given serious consideration by Rep. Boucher's proposed United States Fire Advisory Council. They are as follows:

EXECUTIVE OFFICE: 1825 "I" STREET, NW, SUITE 400 • WASHINGTON, DC 20006 • 202.857.3299 VOICE • 202.429.9
OPERATIONS CENTER: 30 MAIN STREET • ASHLAND, MA 01721-1187 • 508.881.5800 VOICE • 508.881.68

RECOMMENDATIONS FOR THE US FIRE ADMINISTRATION

* Ensure that the US Fire Administration is the major focus within FEMA.

* Elevate the position of US Fire Administrator to Deputy Director of FEMA for Fire.

* Implement a long- and/or short-range plan to give the Federal Fire Program a new direction - a change toward the original intent.

RECOMMENDATIONS FOR THE NATIONAL FIRE ACADEMY

* Regain a position of prominence as the foremost institute of training and education for the nation's fire service.

* Conduct a "reality check" of the curricula and programs of the NFA to gauge the quality, integrity and usefulness of the NFA's work.

* Avoid becoming stagnated by consistently striving to attract - and utilize - the best the fire service has to offer in the line of educators and leaders.

* Shift funding priorities within the NFA to disperse monies at the state level for the development and conduct of state training programs. In the first year of this shifted funding, a total of $30 million in federal monies should be distributed at the state level.

* Reallocate Federal monies to provide funding not presently available at the state level to supplement the purchase of firefighter personal protective equipment. Funding should be at the level of $52 million per year until such time as every active "Hot Zone" firefighter has been provided with a state-of-the-art protective ensemble. Our military leaders would not for a moment consider sending our troops to war without providing them with state-of-the-art equipment to be used in combat. America's firefighters - our domestic defenders who wage war daily against fire - deserve no less consideration.

There has been an alarming deterioration in both the nction and focus of the Federal Fire Programs over the past two cades. Therefore, we support Rep. Boucher's call for the tablishment of a Council that would serve in an advisory pacity to the United States Fire Administrator in looking at e role of the US Fire Administration and the National Fire ademy. It may also be that this should be a permanent advisory uncil with specified membership to ensure equality of presentation.

In further support of Rep. Boucher's concept, we believe that his proposed Advisory Council should also be charged with issuing, each year, a factual and objective report to Congress and the fire service such as the report which the National Academy of Public Administrators (NAPA) has completed on FEMA. Should, for any reason, the Advisory Council portion of this legislative proposal not be enacted, then NAPA should be contracted with to do an independent study of the USFA and NFA.

While the Federal Fire Program needs to be continuously examined from an operational and programmatic perspective, it is essential that an examination of the fire problem in the United States be conducted.

To that end we urge, in the strongest terms, that this subcommittee consider legislation as soon as practical to establish a **National Commission on Fire Prevention and Control, Pre-hospital Emergency Care and Emergency Management** to be appointed by the President of the United States. The charge to the National Commission would be to revisit, review and update the findings of the original Commission - what has changed in the twenty years since the release of the "America Burning" report, and more importantly to provide a road map and guidelines for advancing the nation's fire service and all of its ancillary activities such as EMS and emergency management through the next 100 years.

ISFSI has developed a draft bill to accomplish this purpose and is ready to assist Members of Congress and the Senate to promote its final passage.

The function and purpose of the Commission would be separate and distinct from the proposed Advisory Council. It would be comprised of 21 members and would be charged with completing a comprehensive study within 18 months to identify measures for reducing the destructive forces of fire that continue to destroy lives and property. The Commission's findings would be presented to Congress and the President of the United States.

The recharted "road map" resulting from the Commission's study would ideally include: the use of modern technology (ie. fiber optics and telecommunications) to make training and education accessible to all; methods for reducing line of duty deaths and injuries; suggestions for the standardization and improvement of apparatus and equipment used in controlling fires, classifications of fire departments and recommended levels of staffing for effective response; and recommendations on who can best meet the future needs of the fire, life safety and emergency management community.

The final issue that we feel needs to be addressed is that of proposed funding levels for the Federal Fire Program. We feel that the amount of $31.49 million is inadequate if the Program is to be what it was intended to be in Public Law 93-498. For too long, the needs of our nation's emergency responders have gone unaddressed. The time has come for us to start addressing some of America Burning's original recommendations, and the intent of the authorizing legislation, by making federal money available to enhance the training, education and personal protection of responders at the state level.

Our recommendations for funding are:

* Over and above the proposed $31.49 million, there should be a total of $30 million per year distributed at the state level for the development and conduct state training programs.

* An initial allocation of $2.5 million to institute a funding program such as that already in place within the Department of Agriculture, whereby the Federal Fire Program would fund percentages of the salaries of State Directors of Training, full-time state level instructional personnel and adjunct faculty members.

* Allocate $52 million per year to provide funding at the state level to supplement the purchase of state-of-the-art personal protective equipment for every active hot zone firefighter.

One of the earliest and most successful programs initiated by the National Fire Prevention and Control Administration was one in which Captain Dennis Osmond of the Minneapolis Fire Department went to every state and advocated the value of conducting community smoke detector campaigns.

One of the first teachings of the Federal Fire Program was that individuals should check the batteries in their smoke detectors at least twice a year to ensure that they are functioning properly and will be ready in case of emergency.

Up until now, we - the fire, life safety and emergency management community - have never "checked the battery" of the Federal Fire Program. As we approach the 20th anniversary of the authorization of the Federal Fire Program, we firmly believe that it is time to stop and check our bearings, recharge our batteries and rechart our course for the next 100 years.

National Association of State Fire Marsha

Headquarters
2222 Weathered Rock Rd.
Suite C & D
Jefferson City, MO 65101
(314) 636-4317
Fax: (314) 636-5262

Washington Office
1319F St. N.W., Suite 301
Washington, DC 20004
(202) 737-1226
Fax: (202) 393-4385

Testimony of

the National Association of State Fire Marshals

submitted to

the Science Subcommittee
of the House Science Space and Technology Committee

regarding
The "Fire Administration Authorization Act of 1994"

September 20, 1994

The National Association of State Fire Marshals (NASFM) is pleased to be able to submit testimony in support of the "Fire Administration Authorization Act of 1994."

Since their establishment in 1974, the U.S. Fire Administration (USFA) and the National Fire Academy (NFA) have been a central part of our nation's effort to protect lives and property against the ravages of fire. "The Fire Act," as it is commonly known, was itself a milestone in the history of fire protection in America. In the first place, it marked the entry of the federal government into what had been considered an exclusively state and local issue. Perhaps more importantly, however, it inaugurated a shift in the emphasis of the fire protection community from suppression to prevention. To shift our attention and our efforts from suppression to prevention was the overriding objective of the Fire Act. Today, the relative cheapness of prevention efforts and the relative expense of suppression is a truism -- albeit too infrequently observed in practice -- in the fire prevention community, but we must not forget how recently these truths have been discovered.

Data collection is arguably the cornerstone of the federal fire prevention program, because it is only on the foundation of reliable information that effective fire prevention strategies can be built. The National Fire Incident Reporting System (NFIRS) is the core of USFA's data collection effort. Based on information provided by the states, NFIRS compiles fire data statistics that are used by the federal government, states, and private agencies and associations in fashioning sound fire prevention programs. NASFM applauds the Committee for continuing to recognize the central role of data collection in the federal fire prevention program.

The second mission of USFA established in the Fire Act -- which data collection is in support of -- is, of course, fire prevention. It is unfortunate that chronic underfunding has prevented USFA from being as effective in this area as the authors of the Fire Act anticipated. As is well known, USFA has never been staffed or funded at or even close to the levels anticipated in the Fire Act, and the cutbacks since 1982 have been particularly severe. USFA's public education program, which was originally supported by a staff of nineteen, is currently run on one a half FTEs. The public's scant awareness of potential fire hazards and of appropriate responses to a fire emergency are a direct reflection of this chronic underfunding. Twenty years worth of missed opportunities are too many to enumerate in this testimony, however, NASFM urges the members of the Committee to reconsider the breadth and seriousness of the fire problem in America and the extremely modest budget with which USFA approaches it.

ecognizing the exigencies of recent budget shortfalls at FEMA, NASFM would also ke to call the Committee's attention to a hiring freeze at the National Fire Academy at threatens to leave at least six authorized positions unfilled for the foreseeable uture.

NASFM believes that all four original missions of USFA -- data collection, fire revention, training, and firefighter health and safety are as important today as they vere in 1974. Additional issues, however, may be worthy of greater attention. To nis end, NASFM supports provisions of this Act that would establish an Advisory Council to USFA for the purpose of reexamining the Administration's priorities. NASFM also supports provisions of this bill that would establish a two-year sunset n the Advisory Council. It is to be hoped that the priorities of the federal fire program can be improved by careful deliberation and twenty years worth of hindsight.

Once again, NASFM appreciates the opportunity to give testimony to this Committee in support of the Fire Administration Authorization Act of 1994.